AC/DC

UNCENSORED
ON THE RECORD

BY JEFF PERKINS

Track-by-track analysis by Robert M. Corich
Interviews edited by Michael Smith

C✠DA
BOOKS LTD

C⊕DA
BOOKS LTD

www.codabooks.com

This edition is published in Great Britain in 2012 by

Coda Books Ltd., Office Suite 2, Shrieves Walk, 39 Sheep Street,
Stratford-upon-Avon, Warwickshire CV37 6GJ

www.codbooks.com

Copyright © 2012 by Coda Books Ltd.

Photographs courtesy of Pictorial Press.

A CIP catalogue record for this book is available from the British Library.

ISBN: 978-1-78158-195-7

MUSIC REVIEWS LTD

CONTENTS

HIGH VOLTAGE
ROCK 'N' ROLL

JUST WHEN AC/DC had the whole world at their feet, that same world dealt the cruellest of blows and literally collapsed around them overnight. Many bands would simply have given up the ghost or retreated back into obscurity. Not only had they lost their charismatic front man, recently voted the best of all time in the Classic Rock magazine poll, but they had also lost their talisman and a gifted lyric writer. They had also suddenly been robbed of one of the most recognisable rock voices and a performer whose massive presence and personality was all but impossible to replace. On a more personal and even more painful level they had suffered the loss of a close friend who had been with them from their humble beginnings and who had been a major part of their subsequent staggering success.

Somehow out of this tragedy AC/DC pulled themselves back from the abyss and managed the impossible, producing an album that has gone down in history as one of the classics of all time. The perfectly named Back In Black contained more than just a little of the spirit of the departed Bon Scott and finally propelled the band into the super league that they had been so close to before his death. The album remains one of music's all-time bestsellers, shifting over 42 million copies worldwide. It was everything that Bon would have wanted and deserved. With the knowledge of just how difficult a task it would be to front a band still reeling from such a tragedy, everyone recognised that it would take a brave or even foolish man to even consider trying to fill such shoes. For the band it would be a decision of career-changing proportions.

The band had to get the choice right and once again they turned to Bon Scott to help them out of a corner. Having considered fellow Australian Jimmy Barnes, Heavy Metal Kid's Gary Holton, a singer not short of stage presence himself, Terry Wilson-Slesser of Paul Kossoff's Back Street Crawler and several others, the band suddenly remembered that Bon had once said how much he rated Brian Johnson, who he had seen fronting a band called Geordie when they had supported his own Australian band Fraternity back in the early 70s. They tracked him down and an audition was arranged. No-nonsense Brian arrived complete with his now-familiar cloth cap, then settled in with an impromptu game of pool with the AC/DC roadies before blasting out a piece of Bon Scott legend in 'Whole Lotta Rosie'.

Despite honouring their obligation to audition several more contenders during the following weeks it was Bon's recommendation that held firm and Johnson got the gig. In many ways it can be seen as a sign of their faith in his judgement, even

beyond the grave, but on the other hand there was no doubting that if they were to continue it just had to be the pipes of Johnson that carried them forward. This was a voice that can only have been created by gargling coal and rough whisky washed down with a mouthful of grit. For Johnson, who was in the throes of trying to get his old band Geordie back together, it was a chance that just couldn't be ignored. Initially surprised at their decision to even carry on at all, the fans' reaction to the reports of Brian Johnson replacing the now legendary Bon Scott was an underwhelming mixture of concern and anxiety. How could anyone go on stage and try to replace their departed hero? Could AC/DC carry it off?

A hero is exactly what Bon Scott was to his fans. His stage presence was magnetic. His presence was dangerous, intoxicating, unpredictable, and yet somehow endearing. He connected with everyone, fixing you with full-on eye contact while flashing a conspiratorial grin that would have had you following him anywhere. Stripped to the waist, showing off a body that belied his heavy drinking rock 'n' roll lifestyle, the girls in the audience would love him and yet the guys identified with him too, seeing that he was, at the end of the day, one of the lads. You could imagine him as the guy at the bar sharing jokes, or mending your car or stealing your girlfriend. He could out-sing, out-drink and out-perform a rock world already top heavy with similar contenders. Here was a man living life full on at the very last stretch of the rope. He was just too full of life to be dead.

The shock when the news broke hit rock's foundations like an earthquake. Sure he drank heavily, far too heavily, and had done so for nearly all of his 33 years, but he somehow seemed indestructible. Bon Scott would always be there disarming you with a wink, never taking himself seriously, grinning one minute, snarling the next, while coaxing the very limits out of the band. There was no huge rock star ego in the man and he would often step back into the shadows allowing the schoolboy on speed, Angus Young, to run riot in front of him. His voice echoed the years of hard drinking and reckless living but was perfectly suited to what they produced, an almost Alex Harvey style, the like of which also filtered through into his often tongue-in-cheek lyrics. Anyone who saw Bon Scott with AC/DC will never forget the experience and it is so easy to see him, larger than life, frozen in his full-on glory of 1979, leaning over the front of the stage with the audience eating out of his hands. Such was his presence that the image will not fade.

When tragedy struck it came in a quietly sad and disturbingly lonely way that somehow betrayed his memory as the ultimate party animal and friend to all. If he was to die it could only conceivably be something dramatic. A motorbike accident, the like of which had nearly claimed him once before, some daredevil stunt gone wrong, something high speed, reckless. To die alone, abandoned in a cold empty car by the side of the road, was just not the way someone like Bon Scott was

destined to depart. The manner of his death has subsequently generated years of speculation, not only because the vagueness and variability of the witness accounts, but also in part due to the fans' unwillingness to accept the fact that he had died in such tragically avoidable circumstances. There was a whole story before then of course and the paths that eventually brought AC/DC together stretch across the globe from Scotland to Australia and beyond. It is his life and his living of it that should be celebrated and remembered with warmth, rather than the manner and controversy of his death.

Bon Scott hadn't been AC/DC's first singer and they, in turn, hadn't been his first band. In fact, when Bon joined the Young brothers in AC/DC they had at first considered him to be too old. Bon was fast approaching 30 and was a clear nine years older than younger brother Angus. Ronald Belford Scott was born on July 9, 1946 in Kirriemuir, Scotland. It was the town where the creator of Peter Pan, J. M. Barrie, had been born, a fact that seemed horribly ironic when Bon's death effectively froze him in time's memory, leaving him destined to be forever young as well. He was taken to Australia at the age of six in 1952 when his parents emigrated, and it was here that the Bon Scott that we know really began to form. His parents described him as always cheeky, lively and most of all mischievous. These would be the traits that would go on to characterise his whole life.

He was a tough little Scot in a tough and unfamiliar Australian city. He quickly had to learn how to look after himself. He left school at 15, brushed with authority several times and even ended up in prison. He was of quite a short stature at only five feet five, a fact that is surprising to anyone that saw him up there on stage, but he more than compensated for that by being tough and earning respect among the gangs that frequented Melbourne at the time. He rejected anything and everything that even vaguely hinted at routine and instead chose a path that would ultimately lead him to front one of the world's greatest and biggest selling rock 'n' roll bands ever.

Despite respecting the solid, safe environment that his parents had created for him to grow up in, he also rejected it, and having left school drifted through a succession of jobs. He was a natural drifter looking for something that he could throw his unlimited dynamic energies into. At one point he worked on the docks in Fort Adelaide in one of the toughest environments imaginable for a young man at the time. He also worked on the crayfish boats, undoubtedly another tough and dangerous job, at a market garden and as a tractor driver, but nothing seemed to last very long. He was restless, an adventurer whose subsequent life on the road would eventually suit him perfectly. Despite all of this he also treated people with respect and was held in very high regard by all of his friends, many of whom he remained loyal to throughout his life.

It was music and, in particular, life on the road that would finally fill the chasm in his life. Having learnt and loved the drums from an early age, when his father encouraged him to use his skill and play with the Fremantle Pipe Band, he had already been in several bands. He was in The Spektors, tasted success with The Valentines, then enjoyed a level of local stardom with Fraternity. Such success opened up a whole new world to him, and suddenly music and being in a band was an all-consuming passion that made everything else seem insignificant.

When his parents moved to Perth in 1956, a new phase in his life began that saw him winning awards for his drumming in the pipe band, and appearing on local television, giving him his very first taste of fame. His interest in rock 'n' roll led to a lifelong admiration for Little Richard, along with a quick lesson in how powerful music could be in attracting the opposite sex. He began to perform at beach parties and discovered his voice singing such classics as 'Blue Suede Shoes' and 'Long Tall

Sally'. Moving out of his parent's house, he reappeared with his trademark flaming tattoo just below the line of his jeans.

An important event in the development of a rock hero occurred during his teens. At the age of 16 he was arrested and put before Fremantle Children's Court on charges of giving a false name and address to police and attempting to escape custody. He was also charged with unlawful carnal knowledge, relating to an incident involving a slightly younger girlfriend and for stealing 12 gallons of petrol. He was sent into the care of the Child Welfare Department for two years. It was a tough lesson for the young Bon Scott to suddenly find himself locked away and unable to pursue his interest in music and girls so easily. His parents feared that their move to the other side of the world, with the intention of bettering their children's futures, had backfired. They stood back and watched as their son served his time and emerged a little wiser for the experience. He resolved to never find himself in that position again, and despite never actually backing away from confrontation he tried to avoid such situations in the first place.

His first real band was The Spektors, whom he joined on the drums in 1964. They stayed together for a year in the Perth area before merging with local band The Winztons to become The Valentines. Joining Bon from The Winztons was Vince Lovegrove who was destined to make an introduction several years later that would ultimately lead to the formation of AC/DC. The Valentines were more rhythm and blues than The Spektors had been and drew their inspiration from the English mod bands of the time such as The Who and The Small Faces. The Valentines' reputation quickly grew and before long they performed live in front of 3,000 in Perth. Shortly after, they signed a deal with Clarion Records who released their first single 'Everyday I Have To Cry'. The band was delighted when it reached number five in the Western Australia charts.

In the summer of 1967 The Valentines supported The Easybeats at Her Majesty's. They clearly impressed the more well known act because they gave the fledgling Valentines a song to release as their next single. At the time The Easybeats were huge, particularly in Australia. On bass was George Young, older brother of Malcolm and Angus. Their paths were all destined to cross. Unfortunately 'She Said' failed to maintain the impetus of the first single and faded quickly. Despite this disappointment and to try and pick up their career the band uprooted to Australia's music capital Melbourne, arriving in October 1967, where they continued to gig and build a following. The whole experience convinced Bon that this was where his future lay, and it wasn't long before little else mattered. Life on the road suited him perfectly, but unfortunately would also begin a journey that would lead to tragedy several years later, just as the hard work was finally paying off.

Despite being desperately poor, nearly starving and unable to afford accommodation, it was Bon, ever the optimist, that seemed totally undeterred and accepted their position with

infectious enthusiasm. In truth he wanted nothing else, and for him sleeping in the back of a van after appearing on stage had an intoxicating almost beatnik feel to it that connected with what he needed from life. As long as there were girls and booze he was happy and, of course, Bon being Bon there was more than enough of both.

In February 1968 a further single was released, 'I Can Hear The Raindrops' backed with 'Why Me?'. The single received disappointing sales but increased their exposure, and a relentless gig schedule saw some improvement in the band's finances. It was in the clubs and pubs, some of which were unforgiving to say the least, that Bon learned the art of working an audience. Pelted with glasses one night and appreciated the next, it was a tough and uncompromising lesson in life on the road. A few years later, when Bon wrote the lyrics to AC/DC's 'It's a Long Way To The Top (If You Wanna Rock 'n' Roll)' he had lived every word.

In 1968 and 1969, two more Easybeats-penned singles 'A Peculiar Hole In The Sky' and the more successful 'My Old Man's A Groovy Old Man' saw better sales and a sleeker more produced sound. The year was to prove something of a turning point for The Valentines. As The Easybeats declined, The Valentines grew in popularity. By now they were drawing bigger and more excited crowds and had honed their image to one of a full-on pop group. Bon was told to cut his hair, wear smart clothes and cover his tattoos as the image became almost as important as the music. The image may have changed but they never forgot the rough environment from which they had come. When they appeared before 7,000 fans at Alexandra Gardens the excited audience stormed the stage and the police suddenly had a large-scale disorder situation on their hands. Things got really out of control when singer Vince Lovegrove kicked a policeman off the stage. He was arrested, fined $50 and given a twelve-month suspended sentence.

The next single of 1969 was a bizarre choice. However, 'Nick Nack Paddy Whack' was backed by the first song co-credited to Bon Scott, 'Getting Better'. When they flew back to Perth they were celebrities and were met by nearly 4,000 fans, many of them female. At this stage a downturn seemed inevitable, and just as their Australian popularity was at its highest they were busted for marijuana possession following a search of their dressing room. By this time the music scene was changing rapidly. The Beatles had split up and bands like Led Zeppelin, Deep Purple and Free were emerging. Suddenly commercialised pop bands, even those with a not so squeaky clean image, were a thing of the past. The Valentines' days were numbered. The single 'Juliette', released in 1970, proved to be their last moment in the spotlight as they disbanded shortly after.

Bon was quickly recruited by Fraternity, one of the hottest bands in Australia at the time, as a vocalist rather than drummer and moved into the band's shared house in Sydney. Before he knew it he found himself part of a band supporting American legend Jerry Lee Lewis at the Apollo Theatre in Adelaide, and British bands Deep Purple and Free on their tour of Australia. A single, 'Seasons Of Change' sung by Bon, was released in 1971, which Fraternity followed up by winning the 'Battle of the Bands', officially becoming the top group in Australia. Television appearances followed, one of which featured Bon riding his motorbike, a machine that he was reported to ride naked up and down stairs to entertain the girls. Girls were always a big part of his life, but Bon surprised even those closest to him when he married his girlfriend Irene Thornton on January 24, 1972. A tall leggy blonde that Bon met in 1971, Irene shared his lust for life and sense of humour.

Fraternity signed with RCA and their 1972 single 'Welfare Boogie' sold well. RCA wanted greater global recognition for the band and Fraternity were soon flown off to London in November 1973 to make their first appearance on UK soil at London's Speakeasy club. During their tour they opened for the hard rocking northern band Geordie, fronted by Brian Johnson. Johnson impressed Bon greatly, something he often spoke of, which would lead to Johnson's appointment in AC/DC a few years later. Unfortunately the England experiment failed to help the band take off. London was awash with homegrown talent, and Fraternity returned to Australia only to disband shortly afterwards as RCA and their management shut down the finance. However, while in London, Bon had worked behind the bar in a pub in Finchley, where he was destined to return with rather dramatic consequences a while later.

Upon his return to Australia, Bon got a job on a fertilizer farm in Wallaroo, but he soon began to jam with local band The Mount Lofty Rangers. It didn't go well and following an all-day bender he turned up very late and very drunk, and had a violent argument with the band and his wife Irene. He took off on his huge Triumph motorbike, riding off along the Stirling Highway, where he had smashed up his father's station wagon a few years earlier. Bon hit a car head on. He suffered terrible injuries and was not expected to survive. Never one to do things by halves, he ended up in traction for a month, along with missing teeth, a wired jaw, concussion, and a broken arm, leg and nose. He even spent three days in intensive care, such was the extent of the damage. Despite hardly leaving his bedside, Irene could no longer deal with Bon's errant behaviour, restlessness and unpredictability. The combination of everything destroyed even her patience, to such an extent that the marriage was soon over. Meanwhile, following his recovery, Bon was destined to cross paths with a couple of much younger Scots born brothers, Malcolm and Angus Young.

Malcolm Mitchell Young was born in Glasgow, Scotland in 1953. He was joined by his brother Angus two years later. They were part of a family of eight children, seven boys looked after by their older sister Margaret. Music ran through the family and older brother Alex was the first to form a band. After backing Tony Sheridan, Alex's band later signed to The Beatles' Apple label as Grapefruit. A brood of that size took some supporting, and like the Scott family before them, the struggling Youngs took advantage of the assisted scheme to encourage families to emigrate to Australia, away from the terrible unemployment in Glasgow. The Youngs settled in the Burwood area where, in 1965, another older brother George helped form The Easybeats. Their first single 'For My Woman' was the start of a hugely successful career, with female fans regularly sighted camped outside the Young family home.

The Easybeats were effectively Australia's Beatles, such was their popularity. Younger brothers Malcolm and Angus watched in amazement as George became a star. Inspired by this they both started to learn the guitar. Angus got hold of a Hofner and latterly his now famous Gibson SG, while Malcolm practiced hard on his trademark Gretsch, a guitar given to him by Harry Vanda of The Easybeats. Just like nearly every other teenager of the time they listened to The Beatles, The Rolling Stones, The Who and The Yardbirds, a band boasting a succession of guitar heroes such as Eric Clapton, Jeff Beck and Led Zeppelin's Jimmy Page. While still in his mid-teens, having been effectively thrown out of school just before his fifteenth birthday, Angus joined local bands Kentuckee and Tantrum. He would run home from school, grab his guitar and play, still wearing his school uniform. Little did anyone know then quite where that trait would lead.

Older brother Malcolm also left school early, and while working as a sewing machine mechanic in a bra factory joined a band called The Velvet Underground, the New South Wales namesake of the seminal New York band featuring Lou Reed, Nico and John Cale. They played at local clubs, pretending to be older than they actually were, performing covers of bands such as The Doors. At the time, however, Malcolm was getting into Marc Bolan's T. Rex and began to try and introduce some of their material to the set. Meanwhile George's Easybeats was in decline, and when they came back from the UK to tour Australia for one last time they were supported by Bon Scott's Valentines. A snapshot of this moment in time shows all the paths coming together that would eventually result in the creation of the incendiary AC/DC.

When Malcolm left The Velvet Underground he didn't have to look any further than his own kid brother Angus to start a new band. At the time, Angus was typesetting for a soft porn magazine, but was spending every other waking moment playing the guitar. Malcolm and his ex-singer Dave Evans, whose family had come over from Wales, teamed up and began

to get their own band together. They were both into glam rock, with Malcolm influenced by T. Rex, Dave interested in David Bowie, and both into the glam movement in general. The Third World War was suggested as a name but it was older sister Margaret who spotted the band's eventual name on the back of one of the sewing machines that Malcolm was repairing at the bra factory. The connotations of sexual ambiguity clearly escaped them, and the name AC/DC, born simply out of the electricity that they wanted to create, was chosen. Later when cheekily asked if he was AC or DC, Bon Scott replied, 'No, I'm the lightning in the middle' – how right he was. The symbol they adopted has subsequently become one of the most recognisable in the world.

Their first gig was at The Chequers in Sydney on New Years Eve 1973, during which they played mainly Chuck Berry – a more manic version of whose famed duck walk Angus would soon adopt – and hits by the Rolling Stones and Free. Pretty soon Angus began to develop his wired on-stage persona. One night, having fallen over on stage and finding himself spinning around on his back and yet still managing to play his guitar break, he decided to try it again. The small audience loved it. Dressing up was not unique to Angus though, and other members of the band would appear dressed as traffic cops, a pilot or a harlequin minstrel.

Several early line-up changes helped hone the band even further. Ironically considering Bon Scott's later appointment, drummer Colin Burgess was sacked for being drunk. Larry Van Kriedt also left the band. Then, during a short spell helping out another local band called Jasper, Malcolm met and recruited drummer Noel Taylor and bass player Neil Smith. However, these new additions didn't tie down the rhythm section as hoped, and were soon replaced by drummer Peter Clack and bass player Rob Bailey. In fact, several drummers were tried out, including Russell Coleman and Ron Carpenter. When the band found themselves in between bass players, George would help out, adding his wealth of experience to the very young band.

Through George's suggestion and contacts, AC/DC got a huge boost when they supported ex-Easybeat vocalist Stevie Wright's new band at a free show at the Sydney Opera House on 26 May 1974 in front of 2,000 people. At this time Angus was still only nineteen. As a result of the Sydney show they were signed by Dennis Laughlin, who became the AC/DC manager. A relentless touring schedule was undertaken and the band's all-out assault began to pay off – the following month they signed to the influential Albert Productions, who had a distribution deal through EMI. They quickly gained some recognition and released their first single 'Can I Sit Next To You Girl' backed with 'Rockin' In The Parlour', featuring Malcolm on lead and produced by older brother George and his ex-Easybeat colleague Harry Vanda.

Meanwhile, Angus sometimes appeared on stage in a Superman outfit with the letter 'A' on the front standing for Super Angus, or as Spiderman, Zorro, or of course the schoolboy. The idea for the schoolboy was a reminder of when he used to dash home from school and not bother to change, and was only intended for one night. The plan was to have a nine-year-old guitar hero in school uniform play with the band one night – and then disappear forever. The outfit went down so well that it has remained ever since, becoming as much part of AC/DC's image as its logo. For someone who started in a band called The Velvet Underground, it was ironic for Malcolm and AC/DC to support none other than Lou Reed during his Australian tour.

Despite their shared musical roots, Malcolm and the band were soon at odds with Dave Evans over his increasingly glam stage image. Once Evans fell out with Dennis Laughlin, an exvocalist himself, his time was up and he left the band. He would go on to front Rabbit, who were like an Australian version of Sweet, and eventually went through bands such as Thunder Down Under and Hot Cockerel before going solo. This left AC/DC without a vocalist. Vince Lovegrove solved the problem by suggesting to George Young that they look at the now out-of-work Bon Scott, who was busy recovering after his near-death motorbike accident. The immediate reaction from the Youngs was that he was too old, but when Bon was invited along to see AC/DC in Adelaide he was so impressed that he made it known that he felt he could give the band exactly what they were after. On the flip side, Bon was concerned that they were too young, although he could see what the band could become.

Bon Scott was unveiled as their new frontman at his first gig at the Brighton-le-Sands Masonic Hall in Sydney. The date of October 5, 1974 has therefore gone down in history as the date when the legend of AC/DC really began. The abstinent Angus is reported as being horrified by Bon downing up to two bottles of bourbon, along with some speed, coke and a joint, before taking the stage. But once up there, there was no doubt that the band was finally heading the right way. A two-month tour of Australia was organised, during which Bon began to write lyrics for their first album. When discussing AC/DC's album output it can become confusing, as various different versions were released in Australia to those finally issued in the UK and Europe. Their first album to be released in Australia was High Voltage. With that, the AC/DC that we know were well and truly born. If ever a band had the right name, High Voltage remains living proof that AC/DC did. The album, despite now being more than 30 years old, is a living reminder of the kind of electricity that has energised us ever since.

HELL'S BELLS

THE AUSTRALIAN version of High Voltage opened with a cover version of the classic blues song, 'Baby Please Don't Go', originally written in 1944 by Big Joe Williams. It was some of the record buying public's first introduction to Bon Scott's unmistakable voice fronting AC/DC. The American version did not appear until 1976 and a hybrid European issue, which in reality was a combination of High Voltage and the second Australian and New Zealand album release T.N.T., didn't arrive until September that year, some eighteen months after the album had originally hit the shelves. When it did arrive in the States, on the Atlantic label, it was generally slated and it would take quite a while before they were convinced that AC/DC weren't an 'all time low', as Rolling Stone magazine originally described them.

The album had been recorded in the Albert Studios in King Street, Sydney during November 1974. Angus had caused more than a little consternation when he managed to blow his amp, which subsequently caught fire, filling the studio with smoke. Needless to say the band played on, encouraged throughout by older brother George, as though nothing had happened. Highlights of High Voltage include 'Soul Stripper', 'She's Got Balls' and 'Show Business', a song that Bon used to perform complete with showman's cane and striped jacket. At this time the line up of the band was still in transition, with the drums being covered by session player Tony Kerrante, and Peter Clack and John Proud, who both played on one track each.

Following its release, the band moved into a shared house in Melbourne where Bon was able to fully enjoy the renewed attention he was receiving, especially from the numerous groupies who began to become a feature of the house. It was as a result of this experience that he wrote the lyrics of one of AC/DC's most popular songs 'The Jack'. The title is slang for gonorrhoea, an occupational hazard, that came about as Bon walked around the house pointing out the girls that had it – as he found out to his cost. The house resulted from their deal in signing with Michael Browning's agency. Along with the house came a wage, transport, a paid crew, and equipment to replace the blown amps and damaged mic stands. For Bon and the lads it was everything they could have wanted at that time.

After High Voltage was released the band recruited drummer Phil Rudd. Born in Australia in 1954, in between Malcolm and

Angus, he proved to be a huge addition to their sound. Rudd had been on the circuit a while, having played with local bands like Coloured Balls, featuring future Rose Tattoo singer Angry Anderson. He was renowned for solid, powerful drumming and his addition to AC/DC's rhythm section proved to be a vital ingredient. Still in need of a bass player they invited Larry Van Kriedt back on a temporary basis. Then, when the band appeared at the Sunbury Festival they incurred the wrath of Deep Purple's guitarist, the temperamental Richie Blackmore, and a full-scale fight between both bands and crews blew up in front of the 20,000-strong crowd. The spark that ignited the flame was apparently Michael Browning's decision to put the home band on after the infinitely more well known Purple. Any publicity is good publicity of course, and once again AC/DC's growing notoriety and reputation spread.

It seemed the ideal time to take the band to the UK. A second single, 'Love Song (Oh Jene)' backed by 'Baby Please Don't Go', was released in Australia in March 1975. Turning the record over, the radio stations gave the preferred flip side a lot more airplay. This was closely followed by 'High Voltage' with 'Soul Stripper' on the reverse, which came out in June 1975. The band then set about finding someone to permanently fill the bass slot, trying out Paul Matters briefly before Mark Evans joined. Mark was even younger than Angus, having been born in March 1956, and had gained his experience in several bands before joining AC/DC to forge the powerhouse rhythm section with Phil Rudd's drums and Malcolm Young's guitar. He quickly set about learning his new band's material and hadn't even properly met Bon Scott before appearing at his first gig.

In April 1975, AC/DC appeared on Australian television's popular Countdown. With only seconds to go before taking the stage, Bon still hadn't appeared. When he did, right at the last minute, he was dressed as a schoolgirl, complete with blonde wig, tattoos and a disturbingly short skirt. The band could hardly play for laughing and for Mark Evans it must have been an interesting introduction to what made AC/DC special. The look on Phil Rudd's face said it all. While Angus duck walked, stripped, and rolled around on the stage doing his 'death of a fly', Bon would strut wolf-like and command equal attention through his mere presence. It was a powerful combination and helped make the band a talking point.

Pretty soon the public were queued up around the block to witness AC/DC for themselves. Their first headliner came at Melbourne Festival Hall just as High Voltage had gone gold. It was an event that was filmed for a promotional video intended to introduce them to the UK market. In the meantime the band relocated to Sydney. When the band went back into the studio to work on their second album T.N.T. they took with them stronger material, including the classic 'It's A Long Way To The Top (If You Wanna Rock 'n' Roll)', 'The Jack', 'Live Wire' and 'School Days'. A tour to promote the album was arranged and frequent riots, disturbances and lock outs started to become the norm. A wonderful piece of advertising centred on the slogan, 'AC/DC – Your Mother Won't Like Them'. Bon celebrated this new-found success in his own inimitable way by having another tattoo, jumping into a swimming pool from a dangerously high balcony, riding his motorbike upstairs, and drinking champagne out of a frozen turkey at the King Of Pops television awards. 'High Voltage' the single made it to number six in the charts, while the album boasted sales of over 70,000.

On December 8, 1975 the band hired a flat bed truck and rode through the streets of Melbourne miming to 'It's A Long Way To The Top (If You Wanna Rock 'n' Roll)', complete with Scottish pipers and a bemused crowd of shoppers. This was the song that really encapsulated everything that Bon was all about – the crazy life on the road, the ups and downs, fights and mayhem – and he's clearly loving every second of it. It's a memorable piece of video, catching the band just as they were breaking through, and helped secure a one-album deal with Atlantic, the label that already boasted Led Zeppelin, Emerson Lake and Palmer, and Yes among its stable. They followed this by filming 'Jailbreak', the song that Bon would later name as his best. The video had the band outdoors with Bon standing precariously on a rock as a couple of loud explosions go off in the background. In fact, the first of these leaves the obviously stunned singer grinning at the camera. The film ends with Bon shot dead in a sequence with more than a shade of Jim Morrison in The Doors' 1968 video for 'The Unknown Soldier'.

Their success at this time can be measured by the fact that upon its release T.N.T., an album that appeared wrapped in pair of girl's knickers, sold 11,000 in its first week, storming up to number two before eventually going triple gold. AC/DC was suddenly very hot. To further capitalise on this success the band quickly went back into the studio to work on another album. Dirty Deeds Done Dirt Cheap further highlighted the growing strength and power of the band, but it was time to move on and the UK beckoned at last. The album fully captures a band on fire and in form. Phil Rudd's drumming is deceptively simple and shows how a good drummer knows instinctively what not to play as much as what to leave in. The powerhouse behind the band is at its tightest, driving them towards an end result that has really stood the test of time. Above all else it is the confidence of the collective band that comes through loud and clear. Bon Scott had reached a point in his career where he knew exactly how to deliver a song to its full effect. Angus's guitar was growing in stature and Malcolm had once again come up with riff after riff, a trait that would characterise the band throughout the next thirty years.

The title track had the owners of the telephone number 362436 reaching for their solicitor's number as fan after fan rang it. Next up comes 'Love At First Feel' containing a wonderfully typical Bon Scott title and lyrics. The less than subtle 'Big Balls' is more Alex Harvey than Alex himself, and contains more clever tongue-in-cheek Bon words that are still as amusing today as they were mildly shocking all those years ago. 'Rocker' is just what it says in the title and has Bon announcing 'I'm a rocker, I'm a roller, I'm a right outta controller'. 'Problem Child' and 'There's Gonna Be Some Rockin'' effectively hold up the AC/DC flag, while 'Ain't No Fun Waiting Around To Be A Millionaire' is rather prophetic and ironic in Bon's case.

The album also contains an absolute gem in 'Ride On'. Slow and bluesy it represents an out of character shift of gear for AC/DC and has Bon giving one of his finest ever vocal performances. It is, in short, superb and remains an oft-forgotten jewel in the crown. It begs the question whether there would have been more where this came from had Bon survived. 'Ride On''s inclusion raises this album above its sometimes overlooked status and the line 'Cause I ain't too young too die' brings a lump to the throat and a tear to the eye. 'Squealer' breaks the mood and pitches the listener straight back into a more typical tempo with a sex-fest of wonderfully sleazy lyrics. The album is presented with a now well-developed 'live', in-the-studio feel. It's a sound that isn't that easy to capture, but one that AC/DC did particularly well under the production team of Young and Vanda.

As Dirty Deeds broke, AC/DC performed a show in Sydney, marked by Bon carrying a naked girl who had run onto the stage on his shoulders. The UK tour was arranged, with AC/DC due to support Paul Kossoff's Back Street Crawler, but tragedy struck when the troubled ex-Free guitarist died of a heroin overdose. Nevertheless, the tour continued with Geoff Whitehorn filling in. The band arrived in the UK on April 6, 1976, with Bon hoping that this visit would be more successful than the last. It was a London music scene literally blown apart by punk, with The Sex Pistols running roughshod over the Queen's silver jubilee celebrations. It was an ideal time to arrive in the city for a rough and ready Australian band led by an unpredictably brilliant front man and a demented schoolboy, blasting some of the most powerful full-on rock you could hope to hear.

Playing The Red Cow pub in Hammersmith led to gigs at The Nashville Rooms in Fulham's North End Road. It wasn't long before the legendary John Peel picked up on them and invited them along to record four tracks, which he then helped promote. It was just a matter of time before they made a breakthrough. Suddenly the big UK rock papers Sounds, Melody Maker and New Musical Express all covered the band, and when AC/DC played The Marquee with Back Street Crawler they all printed rave reviews. To celebrate Bon went back to the pub in Finchley where he had worked as a barman. Unfortunately there was a fight going on and as he walked in he was hit in the face by a full beer glass, which gave him an impressive black eye and further damaged his already suspect jaw. By June 1976 they finally headlined The Marquee and kicked off on tour.

When they arrived in Glasgow it was an exciting and emotional experience for the Young brothers, who had of course been born there. Bon went off in search of his roots by visiting Kirriemuir. The Glasgow concert ended with seats being thrown onto the stage when the crowd realised that the band weren't coming back for yet another encore. When they arrived at London's Lyceum on 11 July, Bon was busy celebrating his thirtieth birthday, which had arrived two days before. Needless to say he gave a memorable performance, coinciding with the release of the single 'Jailbreak' in Australia. The tour moved on, taking in Holland, Sweden and Austria before they returned to London to appear on the television show So It Goes, on which

they promoted 'Jailbreak'. On 28 August they were once again in the studio recording three tracks for Marc Bolan's Rollin' Bolan television show, as Malcolm Young's one-time hero tried to resurrect his career. The following day they appeared at the Reading Festival in front of 50,000, along with Ted Nugent and Black Oak Arkansas. It was the first time that the band remember being concerned over a lack of reaction from the outdoor crowd, but this only highlighted the electric effect they normally managed to create.

They became regulars at The Marquee, which had become almost their spiritual home, attracting sell outs of 1,000 several weeks on the trot. With perfect timing the UK album version of High Voltage was launched just as Dirty Deeds was released in Australia. They next moved on through France, Belgium, Switzerland and on into Germany where they quickly built a huge following, supporting Richie Blackmore's Rainbow. The trouble that had started with the earlier Deep Purple fiasco boiled over once again when Blackmore refused AC/DC an encore, fearing that his own band would suffer – and nearly caused a riot in the process. In fairness it was a near impossible act to follow. Following their exposure in Germany they shifted 20,000 albums in a week in that country alone.

When Dirty Deeds was unleashed on an expectant European market they promoted it by headlining London's Hammersmith Odeon before once again going to Glasgow. This time the security was tight and the concert passed relatively quietly – if you can say such a thing about AC/DC! The demands to return to Australia grew and they returned there to embark upon a 26-date tour starting at the Myer Music Bowl. As Angus Young's reputation for stripping on stage whilst still playing his Gibson spread, various town mayors decided to ban the band from appearing, much to the disgust of both the band and their fan base. Their 16 Australian dates throughout January and early

February 1977 would prove to be the last time the band appeared in their adopted homeland with Bon Scott.

With barely enough time to go into the studio to record the next album, Let There Be Rock, they quickly went back to the UK to start a tour, which kicked off at Edinburgh University on February 16, 1977. As a further sign that the band intended to make London a base, the Young brothers moved into a flat in Ladbroke Grove in the west of the city. Meanwhile Bon was staying with his girlfriend of the time, 'Silver' Smith. It would be a relationship that would last right up until the end of Bon's life. Both were rock 'n' roll animals and understood each other to such an extent that the openness of the relationship was never a problem. Suddenly realising that their biggest bands had gone back to the UK, another single, 'Dog Eat Dog', was released back 'home'.

Then, another major European tour supporting the disintegrating Black Sabbath took them back to Sweden. Of course, it didn't pass without incident and at one point Sabbath's Geezer Butler drunkenly pulled a knife on Malcolm Young during a particularly lively argument. Sabbath fired AC/DC from the tour, and this was quickly followed by Mark Evans' departure following disagreements with Angus. The band quickly recruited ex-Bandit bass player Cliff Williams. Williams was older than the Youngs, and being born in 1949 was nearer the age of the old man of the band, Bon Scott, and they quickly formed a friendship.

Born in Romford, Essex Cliff's family had moved to Liverpool just in time for the young Williams to witness the arrival of The Beatles. He worked as an engineer before joining the band Home alongside future Wishbone Ash guitarist Laurie Wisefield. They went on to support none other than Led Zeppelin at Wembley in 1971, but the band later disbanded in disarray, and three years later Williams formed Bandit. When AC/DC made their approach it was an easy decision for him to make and Bandit folded. In fact, AC/DC had held auditions, listening to a number of bass players in a room in a pub in London's Victoria. Williams had been tipped off to use a pick as the Youngs liked that sound, and they offered him the gig, joining in May 1977.

Let There Be Rock was released in the States in July and a tour was planned. Firstly there was the not insignificant problem of Bon's visa application, which had to be sorted out following his earlier drugs bust. When they did arrive they went to Austin, Texas before moving on to The Electric Ballroom in Dallas, a show that went out live on local radio. A slot with REO Speedwagon at West Palm Beach was followed by an appearance supporting the Pat Travers Band in Jacksonville in front of over 8,000. The tour came to an end on August 16 at Madison, Wisconsin. It was the day that Elvis had died and yet they still managed to get the downbeat audience up and rocking.

Sadly, further tragedy in the music world quickly followed, with Malcolm's much-admired Marc Bolan dying in a car accident, and Lynyrd Skynyrd's fatal plane crash tearing a hole in the business. Little did anyone know that AC/DC was soon destined to add to the rock 'n' roll list of the departed. However, Bon was sending out quite large hints that he knew that his lifestyle was catching up on him, and when he was interviewed for the New York rock magazine Punk, he stated that the meaning of life is 'To have as good a time and as short as possible.' It proved horribly accurate.

As AC/DC took America by storm they were invited to open for Johnny Winter, and caught the eye of Kiss frontman Gene Simmons, who booked them to support them in December. When they finally returned to Europe they toured Finland, Sweden, Germany – where the reaction was typically manic – Switzerland and Belgium. It was whilst playing at Kontich in

Belgium that another riot prompted the police to storm the stage, which inspired Bon to write 'Bedlam in Belgium', a track that would later appear on the Flick Of The Switch album. A further single, 'Let There Be Rock' backed by 'Problem Child', was released in Europe, followed by the album in October, which was promoted with another 20-date onslaught on the expectant United Kingdom. October 25 and 26 saw the band play two sell outs at Hammersmith Odeon, not far from the more humble surroundings of The Red Cow pub where they had played not so long before. Another chance to give more exposure to the AC/DC sound came the following night when the band was filmed performing, transmitted on the BBC and radio several days later.

Returning in November to the States to further promote Let There Be Rock, they supported Canadian band Rush in New York State before teaming up with UFO as co-headliners at three more dates. By the time they reached Chicago, for their first appearance in the Windy City, they had received rave reviews, mostly focusing on the manic antics of Angus, the like of which hadn't been seen before, and Bon Scott. Their chaotic showmanship was counterbalanced by the more restrained input from Malcolm's superb rhythm guitar, with the whole riot underpinned by the developing partnership between Phil Rudd and Cliff Williams. Dropping in at the Atlantic Records studio in New York they recorded a live set that the label then touted around for airplay. Opening for Kiss, Aerosmith, Blue Oyster Cult, Styx and Cheap Trick, they further enhanced their reputation of being a feared band to follow, but it was time to record another album, and once the tour had finished they went back to Sydney to start work. What emerged is one of the highlights of the AC/DC catalogue, the massive Powerage.

Recording throughout February and early March 1978, they came up with a set of strong songs containing many of the now familiar Bon Scott lyrics. His clever use of double entendres and his gift for telling it exactly how it is were now well recognised. The opening chords of the album's first song, 'Rock 'n' Roll Damnation', let you know without a doubt that this was going to special. Bon Scott pulls out one of his most powerful vocal performances for 'Rock 'n' Roll Damnation' – and the album doesn't let up from there, moving through classics such as 'Down Payment Blues', 'Sin City', a firm fixture in their live set, and by the time the last track 'Kicked In The Teeth' fades, you feel exactly like the song's title.

'Down Payment Blues' sears and scorches with Malcolm's often underrated guitar driving the song and holding it together, while Bon once again shows his peak form with a vocal delivery that fully justifies his recently voted 'Best Frontman Ever' title. 'Gimme A Bullet' shows a band determined to hold on to everything that they know they can do and do well: balls-to-the-wall rock, full-on, electric, powerful, driven, loaded and yet somehow disciplined enough to really hold it all down. In the studio you can imagine the needles pointing way into the red, as George Young and Harry Vanda struggled to somehow capture the energy on tape, a task which must have been like trying to put the lid back on the Ark of the Covenant.

The album is relentless as it moves through the hugely powerful opening sequence of 'Riff Raff'. Within the cacophony of sound everyone has the space to play, a balance that only great bands seem to find. This is a band at the very height of their powers, leaving you breathless, numbed but buzzing. When played with the necessary volume, 'Riff Raff' is like having the band materialise between your speakers, such is the quality of production. Next up is 'Sin City', as powerful now as the first time I heard it. With the greatest respect to Brian Johnson, who has done such a wonderful and almost impossible job, this track will always be Bon Scott's finest moment. You can see him winking, snarling, grinning, teasing, tongue in cheek in his piratical, conspiratorial, rebellious, reckless, mercurial way. This song is everything that was Bon Scott. If he caught your eye whilst singing it you would sell your soul and follow him right into Sin City. It is Bon Scott personified, a living rocking soundscape of his life, which would end when Sin City claimed him. When he wrote lyrics you knew they were from his own life experience. Nothing fantasy about it at all – this man lived and ultimately died within his songs.

'What's Next To The Moon' and 'Gone Shootin'' struggle a little to follow such a classic, but both tracks succeed at what the band do well, and stick to it without overplaying. 'Gone Shootin'' has the two Youngs interplaying superbly before Bon launches back in and the riff masters wrap it all up in trademark style. 'Up To My Neck In You' – they were never renowned for their subtlety – is up next and opens with another killing riff from the Young factory, simple and straight. It's another great Bon performance that shows a maturity and confidence that comes not only with the strength of material at hand, but also from the tight band playing that their relentless touring had given them. When Bon sings, 'Up to my neck in whisky' you can almost hear him necking the bottle as he sings it. As 'Kicked In The Teeth' ends the album leaving you shell-shocked you just have put it all on again. It is impossible not to hit play.

As Powerage hit the UK shops the band went on the road again. The 'Rock 'n' Roll Damnation' single steadily climbed the charts and peaked at number 24, resulting in their first appearance on the mainstream Top Of The Pops television show. Warming up for the tour they took in Colchester's University of Essex, an event captured on film. A tattooed and shirtless Bon, lead wrapped around his wrist, head-banging wired schoolboy Angus, Malcolm tight up against the stack of Marshall Amps stage left, Cliff Williams stage right, and a pounding Phil Rudd

– energy personified. The student crowd look almost stunned as the decibel level rips holes through those at the front. It is hot, sweaty, crammed, noisy, and everything rock should be. Angus risks permanent brain damage with violent head-banging throughout before launching into his Berryesque duck walk. I have no doubt that the audience hadn't seen the like of this before.

The gig was also the first airing for 'Sin City', introduced by Bon saying, 'If you want blood, you get it.' Off goes Angus, by now melting in sweat, Phil hits the drums with such power that they nearly implode, and Bon gives a typically charismatic performance playing to the camera, the crowd and the band. At one point, Angus in his trademark shorts slides across the stage in front of his brother, nearly flying straight off the other end, tearing painful holes in his knees – now he looks ever more the typical schoolboy, grazed knees and all.

Sometimes you find yourself watching Angus more than listening to him. However, there is no doubt that he is a much underrated guitar player. As rock 'n' roll guitarists go, the Young brothers were a devastating combination, creating a twin assault as powerful as any other band. 'Bad Boy Boogie' is of course the cue for Angus to strip off, leaving him in just shorts and trainers before he gurns his way through his next break. Bon introduces the next song, 'Whole Lotta Rosie', written after a particularly challenging session with a famed Tasmanian lady, by saying, 'This is a song for you about the biggest fattest woman that ever fornicated. Gotta whole lot of Rosie, and so does she.' Then, when Bon introduces 'I'm A Rocker' he pouts at the camera and points to himself. Who can possibly deny that? For an encore they return to the stage and roast the audience alive, with Angus standing on the drum riser before launching into 'Let There Be Rock 'n' Roll'. Presumably the sweat-soaked audience then went back to their rooms to recover.

This tour was also captured on a live album, released in the UK in October 1978 and the US the following month. If You Want Blood You've Got It was recorded for fans to treat their neighbours to a full-on AC/DC live experience. The crowd reaction when the band takes to the stage says it all, and illustrates just how huge they had become. Opening with 'Riff Raff' and moving through gems such as 'Hell Ain't A Bad Place To Be', 'The Jack', 'Problem Child', 'Rock 'n' Roll Damnation' and 'High Voltage' before ending with 'Rocker', it fully captures the live, full-power AC/DC rock 'n' roll event. Stand outs are a sleaze-ball version of 'The Jack' delivered by a leering, Alex Harvey-esque Bon Scott re-living the times in the band house back in Australia, and 'Rock 'n' Roll Damnation', as incendiary as they could possibly be.

When the band took the Powerage tour to the States in June they supported Alice Cooper in Virginia and went on to play a staggering 67 dates appearing with the likes of Montrose, Thin Lizzy, Aerosmith and Rush. The high point in a tour that included some venues that really shouldn't have been on the itinerary was an appearance in front of 70,000 at Oakland near San Francisco along with Aerosmith, Van Halen, Foreigner and The Pat Travers Band. It was a sign that in the States at least they were still considered to be the new scruffy Oz boys on the block, taking to the stage at 10.30 in the morning. Nevertheless, they still managed to ignite the massive crowd and set the day up nicely for the following acts.

The tour started a close friendship between Alice Cooper and Bon Scott, who hit it off straight away. August 4 saw them open for British guitar legend Alvin Lee of Ten Years After and Woodstock fame, and then they returned to Oakland, more than holding their own alongside other supposedly larger bands. The tour was also notable for the band being turned off for playing too loud in Detroit, resulting in Malcolm punching the promoter. By October they were back in Europe doing a further 16-date tour of Germany, Holland, France, Belgium, Sweden and Switzerland. Then, they hardly took their foot off the gas, returning to England to play another 17 dates. How Angus and Bon kept going is remarkable. The band relied on their full-octane energy levels to deliver. Angus of course did not drink, but what Bon was doing to himself on top of this pounding schedule could only really take him one way. When they again sold out the Hammersmith Odeon for both nights it was reported that they could have filled it for a week, such was their popularity. Just as Powerage was going gold in the States it was decided that this was the time to take the band back into the studio for a seventh album.

A switch in producers was suggested by Atlantic, and both

George Young and Harry Vanda were dropped to make room for Eddie Kramer. Kramer came with a huge reputation, built largely at Atlantic, having produced Jimi Hendrix and Led Zeppelin, among many others. He was primarily brought in to give a more commercial feel to any potential singles that the band could come up with. Having broken the live market and the albums selling well, it was a single that Atlantic felt that they needed to generate airplay. This was the era when bands such as Boston and Rainbow were being played endlessly across the States. This decision caused much concern within the AC/DC camp. Effectively, Malcolm and Angus were being asked to fire not only their own brother, but also someone who had produced six successful albums and had played a major part in creating the AC/DC legend. It was not an easy decision to take. George left with valuable advice to the band to not change what they did best: high voltage rock 'n' roll.

The band set off for Miami to start recording – but all was not well. Kramer wanted to introduce keys to the sound, and the band's obvious lack of enthusiasm translated into some out of character, lacklustre recordings. Kramer was sacked and replaced with Robert 'Mutt' Lange. Mutt had already forged a reputation that would later grow through his work with Def Leppard. The band re-located to the Roundhouse Studios in London and began work on what would become their career-defining album, Highway To Hell.

TO HELL AND BACK

'**M**UTT' LANGE was, at that point, largely untried and producing a heavy rock band was certainly new territory for him. Atlantic could see that the band was happy again, and the early tapes sent from the studio convinced them that it was a risk worth taking. Some concern was expressed at Atlantic over the album title Highway To Hell, which was felt to be a touch too far for the Bible Belt lands of the States. However, it was a fear that proved unfounded, and the album became the most successful AC/DC release to date.

The opening track was single material, but before either it or the album was released the band went back to the States to introduce the new material amongst their already impressive set list.

Once again they found themselves heavily booked, with the 53 dates kicking off with old sparring partners UFO on May 8, 1979 at the Dane County Coliseum. May 27 saw them play the Tangerine Bowl along with Boston and country rockers Poco. It was a hard and demanding tour, and they partied as hard as they rocked. For Bon it was the stuff of dreams. The women would literally line up for him and even though the crowds grew and the organisation would plot their every move in and out of gigs, they were still accessible. Bon would not have it any other way. Taking a brief trip to Holland for a television appearance, they returned to the States again. During a concert at the Brown Stadium, Cleveland tragedy struck. A gunman shot a member of the audience dead and injured another before the whole show disintegrated into chaos, with further reports of stabbings and multiple arrests. Then, as a sign of their increasing status, they

played Madison Square Gardens in New York City on August 4, opening once again for Ted Nugent.

By July it was time for Highway To Hell to be unleashed. The live album If You Want Blood You've Got It had now topped 250,000 in sales, but Highway was destined to make that figure pall in comparison. The album soon went platinum as sales took off. Understandably it was with mixed feelings that George Young heard the news back in Australia. The killer title track opens the album, setting a new AC/DC standard and including a wonderful Angus break. Then they take us through 'The Girl's Got Rhythm' and 'Walk All Over You', songs that quickly became regulars in any AC/DC concert from that point on. 'Touch Too Much' became the album's second single, released in time for Christmas 1979.

Other highlights include the full-on mania of 'Beating Around The Bush' and 'Shot Down In Flames', a track that showcased AC/DC's ability to get it on loud and right in your face. Another example of this is when Cliff's bass for 'Get It Hot' comes in and all but shatters glass within thirty yards of the speakers. The radio-friendly 'Love Hungry Man' leads up to the closing track 'Night Prowler', a song whose lyrical content was destined to reappear amid controversy several years later. 'Night Prowler' also provided the B-side when 'Highway To Hell' was released as a single.

The album stormed into the top ten of the UK album chart, and did well in the frenzied rock lands of Germany and Holland, where AC/DC had built a massive and loyal fan base. On September 1 they opened with The Who at the old Hitler stadium at Nuremburg, Germany along with Molly Hatchet, Cheap Trick and the Scorpions. As if they hadn't toured hard enough, they were then booked to return to the States, playing Oakland once again. The endless touring, heavy drinking and partying was taking its toll on Bon, not that he was complaining, and when they embarked upon ten dates with southern rockers Molly Hatchet, his lifestyle was starting to cause concern. It was physically impossible for anyone, even someone as fit as Bon, to continue this pace without a break. September 26 saw them appear with Sammy Hagar before finishing off with more shows with Molly Hatchet in Carolina. This coincided with the news that Highway To Hell had sold 500,000 copies in the short time since its release. Returning to the UK they played four consecutive sold-out dates at the now-familiar Hammersmith Odeon. Such was the demand for tickets that a mere six weeks later they sold it out again for two additional dates. Opening with 'Live Wire', they moved through 'Shot Down In Flames', a tired-sounding 'Sin City', and continued with their usual set.

Moving once more through Europe they played a further 30 dates, including two shows in December at the Pavillion De Paris supported by the up and coming British band Judas Priest. Both concerts were filmed and released as part of the rockumentary video Let There Be Rock. As a 'moment in time' study of a band, very much on the rise, it's fascinating stuff. Powerful live footage is intermingled with some revealing behind-the-scenes sequences and interviews, which sit alongside some almost home-movie style sections of the band relaxing. In one scene Bon walks out onto a frozen lake, in an act typical of why he is remembered not just as a wild man of rock, but also as an eminently likable larger-than-life character.

The Let There Be Rock video is a must-have piece of AC/DC history that shows the band at its customary full-on power. Remarkably, on a musical level at least, it hasn't really dated. The band's image was straightforward and honest, and Angus's antics are as visually captivating as ever, even though they had become so familiar. Bon of course holds centre stage, oozing the kind of charisma that separates a great performer from the rest. The audience was completely under his spell. One staggering thing that comes across is just how young the rest of the band was.

After Paris and the two extra Hammersmith shows the band did four more sell outs with The Pirates – which coincided with the news that their latest single 'Touch Too Much' was giving them their breakthrough on the radio at last – the band took a well-earned break for Christmas back home in sunny Australia. It was to be Bon's last ever visit. Facing another year of relentless touring something had to give – but little did anyone realise just how low the sand in the hourglass had run.

By mid-January they were back on tour playing more dates in England, ending with shows at Newcastle and Southampton. After stopping in Cannes to receive awards for both If You Want Blood and Highway To Hell, they travelled on to Madrid to appear on the television show Aplauso performing 'Highway To Hell', 'The Girl's Got Rhythm' and 'Beating Around The Bush'. It was Bon's last ever live appearance. A press conference was held the next morning before Bon flew back to Paris to record 'Ride On' with his mates in the band Trust. Tragedy was now days away.

The story often told is this. Bon had rented a flat on the fourth floor of Ashley Court in London's Victoria. The flat is in a surprisingly quiet side street that runs off the main Victoria Street by Victoria Station. As unlikely as it seems, its direct neighbour is the huge and imposing edifice of Westminster Cathedral, which is directly opposite the block's front entrance. Just a few doors up on the same side of the road is another residence that attracts altogether different admirers, being where Winston and Clementine Churchill had set up home in times past. It was in this street that the time bomb that was Bon's last night alive started ticking away.

On the night of February 18, 1980 he went out with a mysterious player in the tragedy called Alistair Kinnear. They decided to go to the Music Machine in north London's Camden Town area. Kinnear picked Bon up late in the evening and drove him off towards Camden. Bon was drinking heavily by even his own legendary standards. He made full use of the behind-stage bar and was seen downing numerous large whiskies. At around three in the morning of February 19 they left the club and headed off towards Bon's Victoria flat. By this time, according to Kinnear, Bon had fallen asleep in a heavy stupor. On arriving outside, Kinnear went up to Bon's flat and opened the door using the keys he had taken from the singer's jeans. Leaving the door open, he went back down to the car and tried to get him out. He couldn't lift him on his own and he soon gave up, especially when the outside lobby door was either closed by someone or just closed itself.

Kinnear phoned Bon's ex-girlfriend, Margaret 'Silver' Smith, and she suggested that he take Bon back to his own flat in East Dulwich on the south side of the river. How he thought he would get Bon up his own stairs is not known, and upon their arrival at 67 Overhill Road he found that once again he couldn't lift Bon out of the car, a small Renault 5. He lowered the back of the front seat, put a blanket over Bon and left him to sleep it off. He then went up to his flat and wrote a note telling Bon where the flat was should he wake up and not know where he was.

Kinnear then went to sleep until 11 the next morning, when he received a call from a friend. He asked his friend to check outside to make sure Bon was OK. The friend had a quick look, but apparently could not see him in the car. Kinnear went back to sleep and didn't wake until approximately 7.45 that evening. Kinnear walked down to his car and found Bon dead where he had left him. He drove him to the nearby King's College Hospital – but Bon was long gone. The news moved fast through Kinnear to Silver to Peter Mensch, the band's manager, and on until it reached Angus, who rang around the rest of the band, starting

with Malcolm. Peter Mensch drove to the hospital to identify the body. Malcolm was left with the terrible job of telling Bon's family back in Australia before they saw it on the news. Bon was 33. Death was certified as being caused by 'acute alcohol poisoning', and was signed off as 'misadventure'. As the news started filtering out through the radio and then onto television news, the band was left in a state of total disbelief.

For years the story has become clouded amid speculation about the actual circumstances of Bon's death. Alistair Kinnear quickly disappeared from the scene and did not resurface for some time. Bon's apparent drug use was suggested, but the autopsy on February 22 made no mention of any drugs being found in his blood stream. The autopsy merely reported that Bon had at least half a bottle of whisky in his stomach. The same day, the caretaker at Bon's block of flats in Ashley Court reported finding the door to number 15 wide open. It supported Kinnear's story. Inevitably people wondered how he could leave Bon alone and unconscious in a car, but of course Kinnear himself, despite being capable of driving across London, was intoxicated enough to sleep in until early the next evening.

It is important to remember that this was certainly not the first time that Bon had passed out, be it in a bed, on the floor, or as in this case and several times before, in a car. It was a rock 'n' roll death, with a horrible sense of inevitability about it, a tragedy that had been on the cards for a while. The rock world reported that this death would also signal the demise of the band itself. How someone so full of life had died so alone caused his family, friends and fans much concern. Either way, Bon's death marked the end of an era. AC/DC had achieved their breakthrough, gone truly global, and now their charismatic frontman and friend was dead.

Bon's body was flown back to Australia. His funeral took place on March 1, 1980 following a church service in Fremantle, attended only by those closest to him and a handful of fans. He was cremated and his ashes were marked with a plaque that is still one of the most visited sites in Australia, even today. Many years later the UK rock magazine Classic Rock tracked down Alistair Kinnear, where he now lives in Spain. He told them that Silver Smith had mentioned to him that Bon had been receiving treatment for liver damage at the time of his death, but had not been very good at keeping the appointments.

Malcolm and Angus were too shocked to discuss what their plans, if any, were for the band, and were slightly taken aback when Bon's father told them at the funeral to get another singer and get back out there. He felt it was what Bon not only would have wanted, but also what he would have expected them to do. On returning to England it took the brothers several weeks to get back together. It proved almost therapeutic, even though the gap left by Bon Scott must have seemed impossible to fill. They decided that they didn't want a Bon imitator for fear of becoming a parody of their former selves. They wanted a frontman who was his own person with his own image and sound, who could fill Bon's shoes without being fazed by the task.

For a while Allan Freyer was the chosen one, and was even announced as Bon's replacement in the music press. But, for whatever reasons, both Angus and Malcolm cooled on the idea. Just when they began to believe that maybe the man they were looking for just wasn't out there they suddenly recalled how Bon had raved about the singer with Geordie when they had supported his band a few years back. Geordie had enjoyed a certain degree of success fronted by Brian Johnson, a Geordie himself, through and through.

Born on October 5, 1947 in Newcastle in north-east England, Brian had been working as an apprentice fitter in a turbine factory when, in 1972, at the age of 25, he joined local outfit U.S.A. They were essentially an all-out rock 'n' roll band, and

Brian quickly started to develop his now familiar rasping voice doing a few covers mixed with some original material in the unforgiving workingmen's clubs of northern England. Just after they changed their name to Geordie, the band signed to EMI and released four singles in quick succession. Their first release was 'Don't Do That', which reached a respectable 32 in the charts, followed by the number 6 hit 'All Because Of You'. The next two singles, 'Can You Do It' and 'Electric Lady', released in August 1973, continued that success by charting. Three albums were also released in a hectic period for the band: Hope You Like It, Don't Be Fooled By The Name, and finally Save The World, which all but wrapped up their career. The band split up in 1975, with EMI releasing a farewell compilation album.

To all intents and purposes, that appeared to be the end of Brian Johnson's musical career. Married with two daughters, he retreated to the normality of running a business from a nearby garage, putting vinyl roofs on cars, which was the trend back in the mid-70s. This was his life for five years until he again felt the pull of rock and began plans to reform Geordie. He even went as far as to sign them to a one-record deal with Red Bus Records when completely out of the blue he heard news that AC/DC was looking for him. Being the down-to-earth chap that he is, he ignored the rumours believing them to be just too crazy to be true. Finally the Young brothers tracked him down and Brian arrived at the auditions in London, held in a small room in Pimlico near to Bon's old Victoria flat.

It is the stuff of rock legend that just a few weeks on from fitting vinyl roofs onto old Ford Escorts in Newcastle, Brian Johnson found himself on a plane flying to Barbados with AC/DC, employed as their new singer. The band even helped cover his bills and support his family in order to assist the sudden transition in his life. It was beyond his wildest dreams and with it, of course, came the reality check of having to prepare himself

to appear in front of the rock-hungry hordes of AC/DC fans. Whether they would accept him as the new frontman remained to be seen.

Brian reasoned that Angus not being the conventional guitarist whilst on stage would help, and he knew that he could carry the songs, having blasted out 'Whole Lotta Rosie' so well at the audition. He had come right out of the rock wilderness to join one of the biggest bands on the planet. For Malcolm, Angus, Phil Rudd and Cliff Williams it was a gamble, but one they all felt increasingly comfortable about as Brian began to blend into the circle. The Young brothers also had the basis of what would be one of rock's biggest selling albums of all time, and when they plugged into the Compass Studio in Nassau, Back In Black began to take shape.

Inevitably the absence of Bon would ignite a debate that has continued unabated since the album was released. How much of Bon's lyrics are there on the album? It is a question that the band has had to live with ever since, and one that really doesn't do justice to Brian's contributions. It is beyond doubt that at the time of his death Bon had been working on some lyrics, which he claimed to those closest to him would be part of the band's biggest album yet, following on from the already huge Highway To Hell. He was often seen carrying around a notebook with various lyrics, notes and poems scribbled inside. It is also apparent that his Ashley Court flat was visited just after his death by persons unknown, and various items removed. Certainly the album contains lyrics written in the undeniable style of Bon Scott, but he does not appear on the credits at all. To this day the band deny that any of his contributions were used.

Remembering that the album was released a mere five months after Bon's death and that it took several weeks to find the right replacement, it is little wonder that the debate continues. In the August 2005 edition of Classic Rock, respected writer Malcolm Dome, a friend of Bon's, confirms that he did see some sheets of paper upon which Bon had written some lyrics, which he had said were for the next album. He goes on to point out that some of the lyrics on Back In Black contain all of the Bon Scott trademarks of clever, subtle double meanings, whereas Brian Johnson's subsequent output is in a different, less subtle, style. Personally, for what it's worth, as none of us will ever really know, I believe that the majority of the lyrics were finalised after his death, but the band also remembered and used some of the lines that Bon had clearly discussed with them. All I can say with certainty is that the album heralded a massive comeback against the odds for a band that was still reeling from tragedy.

The album was released in a black cover, appropriately titled, and opens with the tolling of a church bell, before the collective foot hits the gas and an album of pure quality rock 'n' roll unfolds. From the opening line of 'Hell's Bells' squealed by Brian Johnson, this is not just an album – it is a statement of intent. The riff had been in Malcolm's mind for a while and this was the ideal time to use it. Bon would have loved it. The fans certainly did, and Back In Black left the shelves at a rate that was hard for the record stores to keep up with. It was a massive seller, confirming that AC/DC was here to stay and would continue to rock around the world thrilling audiences and leaving them breathless in their wake.

The fans immediately took to Brian Johnson, accepting him as one of the family and respecting his no-nonsense approach and wholeheartedness without question. The opening sequence with the bells is one of the most familiar starts to an album of all time and separates it from the rest of the AC/DC catalogue in the most dramatic of ways. Through it, Bon is remembered. Then the album opens out through tracks such as 'Shoot To Kill' and the cleverly worded attack on the world's oldest profession, 'What Do You Do For Money, Honey'. 'Give The Dog A Bone' and 'Let Me Put My Love Into You' confirm the fact that the band is still as far removed from subtlety as it is possible to be. The title track, 'Back In Black', contains some superb work from Angus, providing a platform for Brian Johnson to confirm his dramatic arrival. The first single from the album, 'You Shook Me All Night Long', follows next, before the rather ironically and controversially titled 'Have A Drink On Me' kicks in. The album concludes with 'Shake A Leg' and 'Rock 'n' Roll Ain't Noise Pollution', bringing to an end a great collection of songs.

Much to the crew's horror, the band decided to take the bell out on tour with them. Not only that but they wanted the bell, literally weighing a ton, lowered from above the stage. It was a huge logistical problem like something out of Spinal Tap. The bell cost £6,000 to produce and was recorded being struck in the factory for the album after the original attempt to record a similar bell that adorns the Loughborough War Memorial in Leicestershire was rejected due to the background noise of traffic and stunned birds captured on the tape. When the band appeared on stage, the bell was lowered, and as it tolled a previously

unknown man in a cloth cap walked forward to become part of the legend that is AC/DC. Their third vocalist had arrived and the Back In Black tour was well and truly launched.

Brian made his first appearance with the band on June 29, 1980 at a show in Namur at the Palais Des Expositions, Belgium before moving on to Holland, where they were captured on film for a concert at Breda. They followed this with 11 dates across Canada from July 13–28, timed to coincide with the album's release. Back In Black roared to number four in the album charts and stayed thereabouts for an amazing five months. The first U.S. gig with Back In Black came on July 30 at Erie, Pennsylvania before they headlined above Steve Marriott's Humble Pie and Sheffield rockers Def Leppard. On August 17 they performed their last ever support slot with ZZ Top in Toledo and then carried on the tour, in Chicago, with Blackfoot opening.

The tour finally arrived in the UK, much to the relief of fans who were, by now, near rabid with anticipation. The band played two dozen dates supported by David Coverdale's Whitesnake and ex-Stone The Crows singer Maggie Bell. They rolled on through Europe taking in some now-familiar haunts including Scandinavia, Spain, France and Switzerland. Two singles from the album 'Rock 'n' Roll Ain't Noise Pollution' and 'You Shook Me' reached numbers 15 and 20 respectively in the UK charts. Sitting on the shelves, meanwhile, was the footage shot around the concert in Paris the previous year. It featured the now-departed Bon Scott, and when it was finally released it proved to be a poignant reminder of times now set firmly in the past. To make it even more difficult it was released on the day that the world woke up to the news that John Lennon had been shot dead in New York City.

Meanwhile, Back In Black's sales quickly reached platinum status. The band celebrated their success by taking the tour, bell and all, to far off Japan before returning to Australia. It was Brian's first visit to the country where the band had started out in much more modest circumstances several years before. At their concert in Perth, Bon's family was in the audience to give their seal of approval, nearly a year to the day after his death. Seeing an opportunity to capitalise on the sales generated by Highway To Hell and Back In Black, Dirty Deeds Done Dirt Cheap was finally released in the US in March 1981. It was a wise decision as this too went platinum within ten weeks of its release. AC/DC was big business and Back In Black continued to shift a remarkable million copies every month as word spread of the band's return. By mid-1981 it had sold over twelve million units. On August 22, 1981 the band appeared in front of 60,000 excited fans at Donington's Monsters of Rock Festival alongside glam rockers Slade, Whitesnake, Blackfoot and The Blue Oyster Cult.

By the summer of 1981 it was time to get back into the studio to start work on their ninth studio album, For Those About To Rock (We Salute You). Mutt Lange once again filled the production chair and the band retreated to Paris where they set up in an old factory. It was not all plain sailing though, and sound problems disrupted recording. They finally emerged with ten tracks that formed the album. Demand for the record proved to be so huge that it sold a million copies in its first week. Eye-catchingly packaged in a distinctive gold jacket complete with a cannon, it went platinum in a mere eight weeks, outselling Highway To Hell and even Back In Black. When the crew, who were still recovering from transporting the massive bell used on the last tour around the globe, saw the cannon they must have known what was coming next. The tour kicked off with a 28-date roll through America and Canada, starting with the band in top slot at Madison Square Garden in New York City. The album itself, released on November 23, 1981 contained enough proof that the band had indeed survived the tragedy of the death it was dedicated too.

The title track is one of the best stadium rock anthems you can imagine, a fact that the band would soon capitalise upon when they took it on tour. It is a nod to the fans who turned up in their droves as the demand for AC/DC tickets outstripped their availability. It also perhaps acted as a tribute to their departed singer, a man who was always ready to rock. 'Evil Walks', 'C.O.D.' and 'Spellbound' have all the power of classic AC/DC. Brian's vocals on 'Inject the Venom' in particular sound uncannily like Led Zeppelin's Robert Plant. The cleverly constructed 'Breaking The Rules' shows a depth to the band's writing. On the inner sleeve of the gatefold vinyl release is a shot of the band taken from the very front row of a concert. Malcolm's huge white Gretsch guitar all but dwarfs him as he powers out another solid riff. The energy and excitement of an AC/DC concert is perfectly captured in that image.

Of course, being one of the most exciting and dramatic live acts around, the band employed two huge cannons on stage, which appeared for the encore. Several venues categorically refused them permission to fire the cannons, but those that did witnessed an explosive end to an amazing show that saw AC/DC reach new heights as a live act. Accompanied by a massive light show, the cannons would explode into life during 'For Those About To Rock (We Salute You)'.

When the band wrapped up the US leg of the tour they took a break, briefly returning to Japan in June, before intending to launch themselves onto the battlefields of Europe with dates throughout August and September 1982. Unfortunately, something was very wrong within the camp and the European leg was suddenly cancelled. Rumours surrounding the health of Phil Rudd abounded, and stories of his battles with drugs suggested the reasons behind the tour being rescheduled.

AC/DC finally got to fire their cannons in the UK in late September and moved through the UK, including four more sell-outs at the Hammersmith Odeon and two full Wembley Arena shows, before moving on to Ireland and mainland Europe. Unfortunately several more shows had to be cancelled when the band hit France. Susan Masino points out in her superbly informed biography of the band, The Story Of AC/DC: Let There Be Rock (Omnibus Press), that by the end of the year they had accumulated an impressive 27 gold and platinum awards in eight different countries. Despite this the band was not particularly happy with the album. Unlike previous recordings, For Those About To Rock had been technically problematic, and despite selling well and being received favourably, they felt that something of their trademark spontaneity was missing in the end result.

Perhaps because of this dissatisfaction they were anxious to return to the studio, and following a break over the new year of 1983, plans were hatched to begin studio work on the Isle of Man in March on yet another album. It was to prove to be an eventful time for the band. Firstly, Malcolm and Angus made the decision, following an expressed desire to return to a more live and instant sound, to produce it themselves. Secondly, Phil Rudd's drug problems had taken him to the point where he clearly needed help. Despite managing to lay down drum parts for the album, his condition led to a fall out with Malcolm, who promptly put the drummer on a plane back to New Zealand to seek help.

The new album was called Flick Of The Switch, and it went straight in at number four in the UK album charts. It was received less enthusiastically in the States, where it stalled mid-table. Flick Of The Switch saw AC/DC returning to the more basic, stripped-down, straight-ahead rock that had been their trademark sound a few years before. Following the massive

For Those About To Rock and Back In Black tours, this whole approach echoed a need within the band to get back to the basics and come up with a less produced, more simple rock album. Moving into the Compass Point Studios in Nassau, Barbados the band worked closely together to achieve just that.

What they came up with is raw, dynamic and invigorating, opening with 'Rising Power' and moving through such quality tracks as the title track, a smouldering 'Nervous Shakedown', a sleazy slow burner in 'Badlands', the out-and-out assault of 'Landslide', and the long-awaited 'Bedlam in Belgium'. Even the slightly predictable 'This House Is On Fire', 'Guns For Hire' and 'Deep In The Hole' keep the momentum going. It is an AC/DC album pure and simple, produced by themselves for themselves, at a point in their career when the band had become bigger than their wildest dreams, representing a necessary return to basics. It was what the Youngs felt was the perfect antidote to the massive stadium rock of recent tours, and the fans loved it.

Following Phil's departure the Youngs placed an anonymous advert in various rock papers for a new drummer. AC/DC fan Simon Wright could hardly believe it when he found out just who he was auditioning for. He had been part of the excited audience on the 1979 tour, seeing the band in Manchester, and was an ardent follower. Wright was chosen, and in a fairytale rock 'n' roll story became part of the band he loved. Meanwhile, back in New Zealand, Phil Rudd was soon on the road to recovery, enjoying his time away from the mania of touring, and started his own helicopter charter company and ran some farmland. It was a world far removed from pounding the drums behind AC/DC, but proved to be just what he needed, giving him the space and peace to sort out his health problems.

Born in 1963 in Manchester, England, Simon Wright became the youngest member of AC/DC, a clear 16 years younger than lead singer Brian Johnson. He had enjoyed only limited success with local band A II Z, who he joined just before their early promise faded, resulting in their break up. To suddenly find himself propelled to the top with AC/DC was the stuff of dreams. His first live appearance with them came at the end of October 1983 in Vancouver, Canada, and when the tour came to an end in the first week of December he found himself at a sold-out Madison Square Garden. Simon Wright's dream come true would soon see him performing with AC/DC in front of a staggering 400,000 people in Rio De Janeiro, Brazil on a bill that included Whitesnake and Ozzy.

The band, now consisting of Malcolm and Angus Young, Brian Johnson, Cliff Williams and Simon Wright, and managed by ex-Albert executive Crisping Dye, who had taken over from Ian Jeffery, reconvened in January 1984 to start work on what would eventually be their eleventh studio album. A typically heavy touring schedule was arranged, which saw the band appearing at several Monsters Of Rock festivals, culminating in another appearance at Castle Donington alongside Van Halen, Mötley Crüe and Ozzy Osbourne.

To fill the gap between Flick Of The Switch and the next album, a collection of previously unreleased material from Bon Scott's days was issued. '74 Jailbreak contained the previously unheard versions of 'Baby Please Don't Go', 'Jailbreak' and 'Show Business', among others. It acted as a perfect reminder of exactly where this now-huge stadium band had come from and the heritage left them by the legendary Bon Scott.

Recording for their new album Fly On The Wall took place in otherwise peaceful Switzerland, with Malcolm and Angus once again dealing with the production. It's another formulaic, no frills but all thrills AC/DC album, released at a time when many felt them to be on the decline – just how wrong can you be? It was an album that would literally shake your foundations.

SHAKE YOUR FOUNDATIONS

BY THE time Fly On The Wall was released in June 1985, Bon Scott had been gone for five years. As much as Back In Black had re-affirmed the band's strength after his death and had proved conclusively, through huge sales, just how successful AC/DC's own brand of high intensity rock could be, it had also proved to be something of millstone. The album had provided the band with plenty of airplay, and the classic tracks were proving a hard act to follow. Sticking to what they knew best was exactly what they did best. This philosophy created another AC/DC highlight with this album.

To support it the band was filmed in a sequence set in a small, seedy New York nightclub. This can be seen on the excellent Family Jewels DVD set released in 2005. Produced by Ian Brown, the album's strongest songs included the brilliant opener 'Fly On The Wall', 'Danger', a track that provides the perfect platform to show just what Brian Johnson's extraordinary pipes could produce, 'Sink The Pink', 'Stand Up' and 'Shake Your Foundations', it is complete with cartoon fly buzzing around from a near death experience to a nearer death experience, including an ill-advised flight into one of the band's Marshall amps. The band start off performing at the Crystal Ballroom in front of an audience of six people and end in typical AC/DC style by literally bringing the house down with 'Shake Your Foundations', leaving them on a stage surrounded by the wreckage of the club, out in the open against a New York skyline as backdrop.

It's good honest rock and makes the next turn of events even more unbelievable.

For many years controversy had rumbled over the true meaning of the name AC/DC, with many Christian groups believing that the initials meant something along the lines of Anti-Christ/Devil Cult or something equally bizarre. When an AC/DC cap was found at the scene of one of serial killer Richard Ramirez's victims, the band found itself deep in a controversy that threatened their hard-earned reputation. It was the start of a series of events that had their critics congratulating themselves over pointing out the evils of rock music. When interviewed, Ramirez had said that he had been driven to committing 16 murders by the subliminal messages contained in some of the rock music he listened to. One of his favourite albums was AC/DC's Highway To Hell and he cited the track 'Night Prowler' as being particularly instrumental in leading to the carnage he caused.

Typically, the band was starting a mammoth 42-date tour of the States when the controversy and subsequent media coverage broke. Several States tried to ban the band and chains of hotels, who in the past had been only too happy to accommodate such a successful band, refused their bookings. When their planned concert in California was banned, several local radio stations were pressurised to withdraw airplay of the new AC/DC album. Sales were no doubt further affected when several shops carried notices warning customers not to purchase AC/DC records, and the new album, along with the offending Highway To Hell, were withdrawn from sale.

Perhaps seeing a twist in the proceedings, horror writer Stephen King invited the band to write a song for his new film Maximum Overdrive. The band obliged with 'Who Made Who', a song that would appear in and title their next album. Concerned over falling sales, despite the perceived strength and justified belief in their recent material, Malcolm and Angus asked brother George and Harry Vanda back into the fold for the next album. It would be the first AC/DC album produced by the pairing for eight years, and the first with Brian Johnson. It was not an album of entirely new material, and along with the title track it contained no less than five other previously released songs, including 'Hell's Bells' and 'For Those About To Rock'. Alongside these were two new songs, 'D.T.' and 'Chase The Ace'.

In January the band embarked upon eight dates in the UK as an opener for a 17-date tour of Europe. On February 27 they were filmed in a live situation in south London's Brixton Academy in front of an audience of Angus lookalikes for a promotional video. Who Made Who was released in May of that year, and despite or because of the older material reached an impressive number 11 in the UK charts, but stumbled around position number 33 in the States. It gave the band their first platinum album since For Those About To Rock. Then, further controversy struck the band when they arrived back in Australia for six scheduled shows. A near riot in the ticket queue for the show at Perth resulted in a reported 63 arrests, and six more people were detained by the Australian police at a concert in Melbourne. The Perth show was again attended by Bon Scott's family.

After the madness of their recent tours, it was once again time to retreat into the studio and begin work on a new studio album. It was to be George and Harry's first set of new songs to play with, and the resulting album, Blow Up Your Video, contained ten of them. The album would give AC/DC another huge success, quickly becoming their best selling album since Back In Black. Blow Up Your Video shot to number two in the UK charts and also provided them with a hit single 'Heatseeker', which rose to number 12. A quick play through

nearly 20 years later fully justifies the public's continued faith in the band and all things AC/DC. Slightly more polished than their previous two albums, it still maintains that necessary raw edge of sounding 'live' in the studio. There are plenty of typically AC/DC lyrics, with the more subtle double meanings sitting alongside those that just slap you in the face. Listen to 'Two's Up', 'Kissin' Dynamite' or 'Go Zone' if any proof is still needed.

March 7, 1988 saw the band take Blow Up Your Video out on the road, starting in the UK with dates at the National Exhibition Centre in Birmingham, before moving across Europe for 20 shows and returning to sell out Wembley Arena on April 13, 1988. By the time the band hit America, Malcolm was suffering from exhaustion and had to be replaced by his lookalike nephew, Stevie Young. The relentless strain of life on the road was once again taking its toll. When Malcolm's alcohol problems became known the band rallied around to help prevent him from following Bon and Phil Rudd. In an incredible six-month period starting in May 1988, the band played a huge 113 dates. Of course, all of these shows were delivered with the collective foot flat to the floor. It is little wonder that something had to give.

Whilst touring they would also work on new material, with the Young brothers continually creating more legendary riffs. And as he recovered his health and strength, Malcolm took the opportunity to watch his band as a member of the audience. He could experience first hand how the band whipped up the audience and worked the crowd, but he also realised, from a more detached perspective, that drummer Simon Wright wasn't quite what he wanted. Simon had received an offer from Ronnie James Dio, and Malcolm took the opportunity to begin the process of replacing him by holding auditions down on the coast at Brighton.

Drummer Chris Slade, who had been born in 1946, the same year as the band's so-called 'old man' Bon Scott, had already proved himself and had attained a highly impressive reputation, with slots at both ends of the spectrum, from Uriah Heep to Tom Jones. He had also worked with Jimmy Page, David Gilmour, Manfred Mann's Earthband, and Paul Rodgers's project The Firm. He joined on a temporary basis, but he fitted in so well socially as well as musically that the position was made a fixture.

Slade was quickly put to work on the next AC/DC studio album, Razor's Edge. It was produced by Canadian Bruce Fairbairn, who had previously worked with Aerosmith and Bon Jovi. As the band's thoughts inevitably dwelled on the tenth anniversary of Bon's death, Fairbairn took the band off to his own territory of the Little Mountain Studios in Vancouver for the sessions. Razor's Edge was rough, tough and uncompromisingly driven – a typical AC/DC album. Opening with the single 'Thunderstruck', a breathless introduction to a full power blast of AC/DC that has become a near fixture in the band's subsequent live set, the album's pace is exhausting. Selling quickly and strongly it shot to number two in the States, and a healthy 13 in the UK. The album contains only a few Brian Johnson lyrics, as he was going through a rather difficult and painful divorce from his first wife at the time. However, he did write the words for the presumably relevant 'Money Talks', which became a radio-friendly single release. Other highlights include the title track and the characteristically AC/DC 'Mistress For Christmas'.

1990 proved to be a year of awards and reward for the band as their all-time album sales rose to a staggering 60 million. Dirty Deeds Done Dirt Cheap was declared to have gone triple platinum and Back In Black sales continued above the 10 million mark. As is often the case, the inevitable counterbalance occurred when a fan was assaulted and killed outside an AC/DC

concert in New Jersey. Even more tragically, at a show in Salt Lake City on January 18, 1991, three young fans were crushed to death at the front of an audience of over 13,000, just before the band took the stage. The tragedy was kept from the band and they performed totally unaware of the loss of life. When the next day's newspapers printed photographs of the band smiling their way through the show with the obvious inference that they didn't care about the tragedy, the band was upset, outraged and totally devastated. Anyone who knows anything about AC/DC will know just how much the band members respect their audience and how much they do for them. Despite becoming hugely successful millionaire stadium rockers, they never lost their recognition of their own humble beginnings. It was the irlowest point and nearly saw the band pull the plug on their live shows.

Fortunately they recognised that it was those very fans that they ultimately owed everything to, and reconvened for another European tour, culminating with a Monsters Of Rock gig in front of 72,000 at Castle Donington. In September 1991 they appeared in Russia for the first time, giving a free show in Moscow before a crowd of an estimated million rock-hungry fans. Returning to Australia and New Zealand for some concerts, they met up with a recovered Phil Rudd for the first time in over eight years. A live album, the first with Brian Johnson, was released from recordings taken throughout 1990 and 1991, and captures the whole AC/DC live experience superbly well. Once again sales were staggering and the single, a live version of 'Highway To Hell', reached number 14 in the UK, resulting in an appearance on Top of the Pops. New York-based producer Rick Rubin called on the band to write a song, 'Big Gun', for the Arnold Schwarzenegger film Last Action Hero. This also charted well in the UK.

In May 1994 the band reappointed Phil Rudd, which led to

the departure of Chris Slade, who went on to work with Asia. Teaming up again with Rick Rubin, the band went to work on another album, Ballbreaker. Showing that they had lost none of the edge that had led to album sales that were still rising impressively, Ballbreaker is a superbly constructed and highly accessible AC/DC album, and one of my favourites. Kicking off with the magnificently simple 'Hard As A Rock', the album continues with all the pace, power and life of any other AC/DC release. With Rudd back in the chair the chemistry is tangible, and the band pull out an album that sits among the best of their considerable output. It is as sleek and stripped back as the girl in Brian's 'Cover You In Oil' will ultimately become by the time the second track finishes.

They then took Ballbreaker out on tour, with 48 dates in America, followed by further dates in Chile, Argentina and Brazil, where they played in front of 65,000, which once again helped to underline the band's commitment to the cause. The tour finally wound up in Australia, and after several months of hard work ploughing through hours of old tapes, the Youngs finally released the Bonfire boxed set. The five-disc set, which went on sale on November 17, 1997, proved to be the ultimate memorial to their fallen friend, and came complete with a guitar pick, bottle opener, poster, sticker and Bon Scott tattoo. It went gold within days. Meanwhile, Back In Black was now fast approaching 20 million sales before going diamond in March 1999.

Despite enjoying everything that such success can bring, the band amazingly still had the drive and energy for another studio album, Stiff Upper Lip, their seventeenth. This time George Young returned to the producer's chair without his long-time partner Harry Vanda. Originally called Smokin' until someone reminded them that Humble Pie had already done that, Stiff Upper Lip was released in February 2000, continuing from where Ballbreaker left off. It rose to number one in the album charts and went gold and later platinum across Europe. For the tour the band commissioned a 40-foot tall brass Angus, complete with horns, which stood centre stage before the real Angus arrived to deliver his customarily eccentric brilliance. By this time Angus had reached 44 and Malcolm 47, but they still somehow maintained the pace that carried the brass Angus through 34 American dates.

During the Stiff Upper Lip tour the band put in an extra appearance to leave their handprints in the Los Angeles Rock Walk Of Fame on Hollywood Boulevard. Moving on to Europe, a further tragedy occurred when a 38-year-old fan fell to his death from a balcony as the band played Gent in Belgium. The

Europe tour ended in Barcelona on December 14, 2000 and they celebrated the new year by going back to Australia for a further 15 shows. Their arrival back 'home' was marked by the press announcing that AC/DC had now sold over 70 million albums since setting out on that open-top lorry all those years ago. It was a remarkable rags to riches story. Whilst Brian Johnson was busy building a life-size replica of his much-missed Newcastle haunt The Queens Head pub in his home in Florida, the rest of the band took a breather before once again launching themselves before a hungry public.

Continuing at a pace that was typical of their entire career, the band toured Europe once again in 2003 with 15 open-air dates, including the UK's Milton Keynes Bowl, a gig that attracted rave reviews. Bon Scott was finally recognised by his birth town of Kirriemuir when a plaque was unveiled to him in Cumberland Close, and back in Australia his grave in Fremantle was declared a national heritage site and continued to be one of the most visited places in the country. The band was inducted into the Rock 'n' Roll Hall Of Fame following a campaign by Billy Joel, among others, and they received the award from Aerosmith's Stephen Tyler. In response, Brian read Bon's lyrics to 'Let There Be Rock' – it was a moving and fitting tribute. Meanwhile, Angus and Malcolm appeared on stage with the Rolling Stones in Sydney and were invited back to appear with them again for three dates in Germany and in front of 500,000 people in July 2003 in Toronto, Canada at the country's biggest ever event. When AC/DC returned to their old stomping ground of the Hammersmith Odeon (now Apollo), the concert sold out in an incredible four minutes over the Internet.

Back In Black album sales continue and have now reached a truly incredible 24 million as new generations of rock fans all over the world latch onto the legend that is AC/DC. Two streets have been named after the band in Spain's Madrid and back in Melbourne in honour of everything they have achieved. The Australian AC/DC tribute band Riff Raff marked the 25th anniversary of Bon's death by re-enacting the open-bed truck drive through Melbourne performing 'It's A Long Way To The Top (If You Wanna Rock 'n' Roll)'. The lyrics to that song, brilliantly written 30 years ago, prophetically tell the whole story of AC/DC. It proved to be a long way indeed – but they did reach the very top. In the face of both triumph and tragedy, their belief and commitment to rock 'n' roll has survived all the tests that life could throw at them. It was just reward for one of the hardest rocking and hardest working bands in the history of music.

It has to be remembered that it was never going to be an easy ride. Just as Bon sang as the band drove through the streets of an unsuspecting Melbourne on the back of a truck all those years ago, 'I tell you folks – it's harder than it looks.' He was so right – but they got there all the same. Gone, but never to be forgotten. Bon would have been so proud of them.

THE INTERVIEWS

I T IS both a tragic fact and a moribund irony that in the rock world the death of an artist often represents his coup de grace, his emergence into the public eye and entry into the unofficial music hall of fame. Such was the case with Bon Scott; former lead singer of Australia's AC/DC. For five albums the band struggled to secure a foothold, but it wasn't until his untimely and disheartening death on February 19, 1980 that the band managed to gain just that.

The conversation that follows here took place just after the release of Highway To Hell, Scott's final album. Bon, who was as fiery offstage as he was on, was a colorful talker and not one to mince words. He was a rebel in his own way, living an exaggerated life that used no clocks, and paid little attention to tomorrows. The band's onstage performances were the perfect vehicle for Scott's manic antics and at any concert one could see him bare-chested, sweating, singing like the possessed, gradually turning AC/DC into the act it would eventually become.

The band had only just walked off the stage at one of Bill Graham's famous Day On The Green concerts in Oakland, California, when Bon and guitarist Angus Young were cornered. Sipping beers and still flying high on the adrenaline rush from a chilling performance, the pair was sequestered for a few minutes. This interview may not offer tremendous insight into the persona of Bon Scott – he was well liquored up at this point and exploding with energy – but it does show that even to the last, he went out kicking like hell.

What are your feelings on the new record?
Angus Young (AY): I think it's great.

The best you've done?
AY: Fuck, yeah. We spent a lot more time on this one. A lot more people are listening to the band than ever done before.

What is the process like when you record in the studio?
AY: They get me and they strap me to a seat and then say, 'Go play.'

Bon Scott (BS): When we record everybody thinks with one mind. Everybody gives suggestions and says, 'Why don't we try this?'

Do you run around the studio when you're cutting guitar parts?
AY: Yeah. I don't know too much about the technical side of guitar; I never bothered with it. If you know too much, it all becomes complex and then you start dissecting and analyzing. I just like thinking of it as good clean fun, you know? The only times I pick up a guitar is when I feel like playing, rather than doing six hours a day practice.

Where do the ideas for the songs come from?
AY: We pick up riffs and things on the road. You might come across somethin' and it sticks in your head. We don't just walk in and go, 'Well, we've got nothing, what are we gonna do?', then all sit around and twiddle our thumbs. We always have a good idea.

How would you say the band has developed since the first two albums until now?
AY: Oh, the band has come a long way.
BS: And the fact that our music hasn't changed...
AY: The band has a lot of rawness. It's progressed, but it hasn't lost its feeling.

BS: No matter how long you play rock and roll for, the songs might change, just as long as it's still got balls!

AY: A lot of people take us wrong; people criticise us because they say we can't play. It's a lot of bullshit.

BS: Shit, man, we could play fuckin'…

AY: Two hundred chords.

BS: Anything, jazz, whatever. But we choose to do what we do. Anybody who criticises that is themselves thinking wrong. We're not wrong-thinking, they are.

AY: I hate bands that go above people's heads, you know? Musically they're trying to put shit on an audience. They're not going with 'em, they're going against 'em.

So people like John McLaughlin and Al DiMeola bore you?

AY: Fuck yeah. If I wanted to sit down and play like John McLaughlin, I could. It would be a piece of shit to me.

Do you listen to any other music?

AY: No, not really.

What about other guitar players?

AY: Not if I know I can do it myself. I like watching flamenco guitarists. People say, 'Listen to this' and it just sounds like the guy next door. There are a lot of good guitarists in the world, but I just lose interest. It's like if you saw Pete Townsend when he first started off, it was all bang, bang the hell out of the guitar. But the style he plays is probably the most imitated in the world. Eric Clapton was happening but he got too technical. He made 12 bars seem like a big thing. There are a hell of a lot of good players around, so many you can't keep track. I haven't bought a record in years, except some things by Muddy Waters.

So you were aware of people like Clapton and Jeff Beck and Jimmy Page?

AY: Yeah, they've been ripping me off for years. At the time I was playing, these were all the people who were famous. Jeff Beck I don't know about; all I ever heard of Jeff Beck was when he played rock and roll, I don't know what he's doing now. And Jimi Hendrix was an entertainer. He was on The Old Grey Whistle Test (television program) in England and he was playing Wild Thing or something like that, and all that was was fuckin' noise.

How do you feel about punk bands? Any sympathy for them?
AY: None.
BS: What's a punk band?

In 1977 AC/DC made their first live forays into the American market, supporting REO Speedwagon, Moxy, Kiss and Blue Oyster Cult along the way. One of the acts they encountered was British proto-metal outfit UFO, which had just recorded the breakthrough album Live Wire. The two bands soon became friends and by 1979, the year of AC/DC's breakthrough album Highway To Hell, they were playing together on a regular basis.

The following is an exclusive interview with UFO bass player and founding member Pete Way in which he recounts his time on the road with Bon Scott, Angus Young and the others, remembering the effect their music had on him, and reflects on the events surrounding Scott's tragic passing on the 19th of February 1980.

So how did you come to meet AC/DC? When did you first bump into them?

Pete Way (PW): I first bumped into them, so to speak, on the television screen. I saw them play, I think it was 'Jailbreak', on some TV program and I thought "I gotta go and see them". So I went to the Marquee Club [in London] and I met 'em. And it was, well, brilliant. I thought "this is exactly the type of music that I like". They didn't seem to care where the chorus came, or worry about where the lead break was, the music just came at you like a train. So I went backstage and introduced myself. They didn't know or care who I was! But we got talking and became firm friends.

What year was that, Pete?

PW: Oh my god – 1912 or something. It was the early days when they first came over [from Australia]. I met Angus and Malc and Bon and they were just real nice people, y' know? We kind of bonded I guess.

And how did they fit in with the scene at that point? What did everybody else think?

PW: I think everybody was like – "wow!" It was rock and roll, wasn't it? It was something different. But then again, as a rock musician myself, it was everything I liked doing. It was everything I'd have liked UFO to have done.

I've heard that a lot of people thought that they were kind of punkish.

PW: Yeah, it had that element didn't it? They had that in-

your-face thing, y' know? I mean, there were other bands that had done that, but AC/DC, they were their own band. I don't suppose they even cared what the new Sex Pistols single was, or about The Damned, Yes, or Led Zeppelin – well maybe Led Zeppelin. But, no, it was music that was original, it came from somewhere other than England and it hit you in the face. "We're AC/DC and you'd better watch us!"

Were they living in London? Did they all live together?
PW: Yeah, they did live in London. I didn't visit them at the time. But they were playing at the Marquee regularly and I would go and see them. I got to know them, and I'd go into their dressing room with all that, "Hi how are you doing?" stuff, but I was also a fan; I loved the music.

So how did they come to be on tour with UFO? They supported you, didn't they?
PW: UFO became popular in America, and we got to the stage where we were playing quite big venues, y' know, several thousand people. We did certain shows [in 1977 and 1978] with Foreigner headlining, us as special guests, and AC/DC - it being their first American tour, opening the show. I watched their set every night – they were in-your-face - just a great rock 'n' roll band. UFO would go down better than Foreigner, so what happened was, since we were closer to real rock 'n' roll, and AC/DC certainly were, we ditched Foreigner [in 1979] and did a UFO and AC/DC tour with 12,000 people every night!

Yeah, I heard that Foreigner was absolutely horrified when AC/DC came along?
PW: Yeah, well, it was more their road crew. AC/DC wasn't a pop band, and neither was UFO. They just didn't get it.

In fact I think Bon sang about being Cold As Ice [on 1976's 'Problem Child'] before, didn't he? Before Foreigner did, I think [Foreigner's hit came in 1977]

PW: Yeah.

What was it like being on that tour with AC/DC? I mean, was it all just a big laugh? Were they just good blokes?

PW: Well, that was probably our eighth American tour, or something like that, and we virtually lived in America, in and out of suitcases, and in and out of Los Angeles. With AC/DC, it being their first time in, it was great. What the agency did when they put the two bands together really made sense. AC/DC was a great opening band. They'd do sixty minutes in-your-face, then we'd come on and do something with more dynamics, and it was brilliant. It went across America really, and it worked. I can't remember the second part of the first part of the question...

Yeah, it doesn't matter.

PW: Well yeah, we had a lot of laughs, we'd have a few drinks! You'd see Malcolm in the bar - Malcolm doesn't drink anymore - but you'd see Malcolm in the bar... we had a good time. Angus always drank tea...

What were Angus and Bon like on stage?

PW: Angus had tremendous respect for Bon. Angus was Angus, you know? But the whole thing was a sort of chemistry. If you were to use Foreigner as an example, probably the wrong example, but anyway... you got Mick Jones writing the songs – "it was the coldest night I saw" – or whatever, you know 'Hot Blooded' or something. When Angus or Malcolm wrote something, and Bon put his words to it, he put all of his energy into the song and the whole thing sparked and became really special. And they played as loud as they liked, which was something that I really admire! With UFO for instance, and UFO were pretty successful, but we'd still have our sound engineers going, "Keep it down, Keep it down". But when AC/DC would go on, and they didn't keep it down at all, we'd go, "I wanna be with the blokes who don't keep it down!"

Did you ever get to play with them, did they jam much? Were they that type of band?
PW: No. In actual fact I spent several evenings with Angus over those months, and Angus would never jam, didn't wanna jam, just wasn't interested. Most people, if you go for a drink... well, Angus wouldn't have a drink, he might have a soda or something, or a cup of tea at the most. I would always ask him, "Are you getting up, Angus?" and he'd always say "No" because he didn't see jamming. The way Angus played was Angus, it was AC/DC, that's what he played. There were no two ways about it.

Do you think that's because they were quite formulaic in their own, wonderful way?
PW: Well, what's Angus gonna do? Get up and play the blues? Of course he could have, but he didn't. He's done his show, done his job and he's lived and breathed it, loved it.

And what about Bon's lyrics – where do you think he got them from?
PW: Well, he's a poet isn't he? A modern day poet. Long before [Motley Crue's] Nikki Sixx decided he was a street poet, Bon was writing the script. He wrote about life, and it's brilliant because you can laugh and you can cry, but you really get an insight. Bon's lyrics were so raw, and got right to the heart of that music.

I like the way that he was just singing about his life and stuff that was happening around him.
PW: Well, let me tell you this - I'd sit with Angus, talking about Foreigner, and Angus would go, "So fucking what? Who cares? They don't play my fucking rip". I mean for me, a lot of it was

like Chuck Berry played loud or that sort of a thing - it was the intensity of it, and Bon lived up to that, he was great. He was the Freddie Mercury of hard rock, and whereas Freddie did the camp thing with Queen, Bon Scott was the president of hard rock.

It's weird, because as far as I can gather, they only really hit the big crowds and everything from that tour they did with you? Did you realise that at the time?
PW: Well, sadly, it was only after Bon had passed away, after Back In Black came out, that they became very popular. When Highway to Hell was released it was obviously a very well done album, with [producer] Mutt Lange doing a great job, and it showed all of their potential, a little bit like when we had Ron Nevison do Lights Out, which kind of broke us. They always had that potential, and then of course when Bon went, they focused on making an album that was really good. The quality had always been there. What was beautiful about the AC/DC thing was that they never put themselves in a situation like some bands do and say "We've gotta write a hit single. Where's the chorus? Where's the this, where's the that?" Instead, they go "No, we're AC/DC; this is the way we're playing".

It's hard to think of any bad tracks they did really.
PW: I think that now and again they might have gotten into the syndrome of 'being AC/DC', but it's difficult not to do, you know? But at the same time, say with Brian, how do you follow Bon Scott? Brian did it very, very well in a very difficult situation. Brian just came in and said, 'I sing. I've just got this voice but I like your boys' style'. You could probably have Cliff Richard come in and sing. He'd probably sing 'Whole Lotta Rosie' quite well! The band was always, 'We don't give a shit. We fucking play the way we play'. And that's the thing. If you like, their relevance to punk is all to do with the attitude - if you know you're good then you know you're good. It's all about confidence.

A lot of the lyrics on Back In Black were written by Bon, weren't they?

PW: Yeah.

Do you think that's why it might work so well? The combination of Bon's lyrics and Brian's delivery?

PW: Well, it's difficult to say because I think that Malcolm Young's melodies were still there, because obviously Malcolm and Angus were writing the songs, and they knew how it worked, and Brian attacked it in a similar way, with his tongue firmly in his cheek. How can you make it work if you change the style of singing? It's like the chicken or the egg. Is it the guitars that make it, or is it the vocalist that makes it? Poor old Cliff or Barry Manilow ain't gonna be able to sing for AC/DC, are they? I could tell you stuff about them as well, 'cause their management offices were above AC/DC's management offices...

I heard that AC/DC got pretty angry when they didn't get the promotion or billing that they felt they deserved? Like on the Foreigner tour...

PW: Yeah, but it's great to be big when you actually do it from scratch, you know? You can get any producer in the world, you can get record companies' advice. They'd get advice and they'd say, 'No, this is what we do'.

What do you think was good about those years? The Bon Scott years seem like such a long time ago...

PW: Well, like Elvis Presley, you go back to things like that. I mean, Elvis's backing band, how would they get a new Elvis? It's like that. But you know what? You can't take it away from Brian, because Bon wasn't coming back. The thing was, it was the character and the charisma, and the charisma stayed the same, the attitude stayed the same, and the fans loved all that. But Bon was an innovator. I mean, let's be honest, when AC/

88

DC were still trying to get Top 30 albums, there were singers like Robert Plant, with his huge vocal range. Where was Bon's vocal range? He could sing, but he was closer to Alex Harvey, who I admire a great deal. He was more that sort of thing. He had that attitude. Angus had a guitar sound that Jimmy Page didn't, and it's as if they were in a different dimension. Bon was like a, "Bang, bang, bang, bang, bang;' an Alex Harvey-type from Glasgow. That's the way I see it, anyway.

I suppose that's the thing about AC/DC, the attitude?
PW: Could you imagine if Bon had decided to try and sound like Robert Plant? Or Roger Daltry? Or Mick... well, Mick Jagger's probably closer.

You know the drummer? Did you know him very much?
PW: Phil? Yeah. Of course.

He always looks like he's not really with it when he's playing!
PW: It's the intensity that Phil had; yeah, you know what I mean?! That's the beauty of the rhythm section - they just sit there, perfectly tight. I said to Malcolm one day, I said it goes back to the Credence Clearwater thing, going back to the early days when the rhythm was so tight that the guitars can do whatever they like over the top. A little bit like UFO, where Michael Shenker could play across the top of a real tight rhythm fill. That's what you do. Watch Michael or Malcolm play. If you watch Malcolm Young play that tight (mimics playing), the whole thing is so intense. It gets so intense, real loud, right in your face, and off goes the singer!

I suppose that's the key to it really, that they're really solid.
PW: But it's the only way to be. I mean, all the best bands were solid, y' know?

They've been criticized, I think, for the rhythm section just sitting there, hanging back. Not criticized, but ...
PW: No, they don't hang back, they never hang back - ever -

that's the one thing they never do. It's so immediate, and off goes Angus and the vocals. It's that thing. They were Giants. Still are.

Did they used to go out into the crowd very much on those American Tours?

PW: Yes, I've seen Angus, he'd have to come back, 'cause his satchel exploded and things like that. And he'd have to get back quick...

What was it like when you played all those small towns? Were the audiences receptive?

PW: Oh yeah, it was AC/DC, man! I mean, we were the known band at the time. 'Too Hot To Handle' was getting radio play, but AC/DC wasn't on the radio. So when people came in at 8 o'clock and they saw AC/DC, they'd be taken by surprise – 'wow!' They'd instantly identify with it because they'd come to see UFO, a band that was still rock 'n' roll, but more subtle in their approach. When you've got something that's so in-your-face to start with, it makes for a great night. Oh yeah, believe you me, Springfield, Illinois and places like that. You know, the beauty of it was that we'd be doing places where Journey had been the day before, or two days before, or whatever. And they'd have like 6,000 and we'd have 12,000. That's with AC/DC. We carried the flag.

What was it like after you all came off stage? What was the atmosphere like?

PW: We normally went back at the hotel and got together in the hotel bar. That sort of thing.

But I mean, is that when you all got to know each other?

PW: No, you'd see each other every night. I mean, I'd always go and see them before they went on 'cause I used to liked to stand and watch them play, it was an enjoyable experience. I mean, what else are you gonna do with your evening? You wanna go and watch AC/DC play, or you wanna go and sit in the hotel bar? No, you go and watch Angus and the boys, get an education in rock and roll.

And what about the last few times you saw Bon? Was there any indication that he was perhaps...?

PW: No, not at all. Let's look at things like this. People talk about binge drinking and things like that, but Bon was on top of his game. I remember Angus going, 'Yeah, Bon's been drunk three times today'. Well, I drink quite a lot during the day you know, and I know I shouldn't, I don't want to. I think what happened with Bon, a terrible thing happened, and I think that there might have been drugs involved because he was at a show at the Hammersmith Odeon and there were drugs around. But Bon wasn't somebody who was looking to get high. Bon drank, simple as that. So no, there was never anything like that. You gotta remember, when you're touring, you have a certain lifestyle and we were young enough. You get back to the hotel and you say, 'See you down the bar'. Simple as that. No big deal. Yeah, a few lines of coke or whatever, the usual thing. One of the best things Angus ever said to me was, 'People ought to give up that stuff and have a good breakfast'. I'd have the same bank account as Angus, perhaps. But no, you know, when you're on the road for two years and you're in a hotel, you get back from the gig and you hang out and you have a laugh. It's actually not just having a laugh; it's almost like winding down.

I can understand. It's so energetic on stage, isn't it? You need to calm down.

PW: I'll tell you the other thing about being on stage. I think with both bands - nobody ever went on stage so drunk that they couldn't perform. It wasn't like days of grunge or whatever, where people took that form of style onto the stage, like it's an art form to be fucked up. It was never an art form to be fucked up. We were playing high energy music and it was the adrenalin that was getting us there.

That's what they always said about Bon – nothing ever interfered with his performance.
PW: No, exactly. I mean, all the best players, to a certain extent, can take certain things - but you know when to stop. The worst thing is if you get caught out. He wasn't working the day he died, he had a day off. For people that like to work, a day off is a disaster – they're thinking, 'I should be on stage'.

Was it a shock because Bon wasn't a person who was out of control?
PW: Nobody thought they were out of control. Nobody thought that they, that anybody, was out of control. In our circle of friends, if we used, we used. To us, junkies were people who couldn't work, you know? They were just drug users who supplied; they were dealers, or whatever. For us, a bar, a drink; it was a lifestyle. If you can't play, you can't be in; you can't live your dreams, can you? And we were able to live our dreams.

So what were your favourite AC/DC tracks at this time? What do you think was a real belter?
PW: I don't really know. Just about every song that they ever did!

That's what's so difficult with making this book because everybody... you know, normally we have to say which single was a real hit, which was a floor filler ….
PW: It doesn't really matter. We could go and put a bunch on now and it wouldn't really matter which one was better. How do you say what's the best? You can have 'Long Way To The Top', or 'Highway To Hell', you can have 'The Jack', you know - what's better? It's like the Rolling Stones. I mean, do you say 'Honky Tonk Woman' or, I dunno, 'Ruby Tuesday'? You know

what I mean? Led Zeppelin, what's the best one? 'Stairway To Heaven', 'Whole Lotta Love' – it doesn't come into it. It's a style, it's a creation; it's art.

Did you guys ever play with the Johnson-fronted AC/DC?
PW: No, never. By that stage, AC/DC were much bigger than us anyway. They deserved to be, you know? Brian did it very, very well. Of course for me, they were always excellent, they were always there. It's like the Elvis Presley thing. When he came along, Elvis was just a little bit more special than all the people that... you know what I mean? I'm not knocking UFO, because I know that there's a great deal of UFO stuff that people like, but if you wanted a band that actually did something, and knew that other bands would never go down that path, and would never go, 'Oh hang on a minute, where's the bridge? We need a slow bridge!'... there was no slow bridge with Angus and the boys, there was no sing-along bit. Well, I suppose 'Highway to Hell' is a sing-along! But you know what I mean, I like that. No compromise. It's like early Van Halen - no compromise.

Do you think the band took a lot of flack for bringing in Johnson so soon?
PW: I think they had two choices, really. I mean, what are they gonna do? Wait around for a year even though they've got an album already written? Apparently they were thinking of breaking up. How do you break up? Or do you just do what comes naturally? You carry on playing. With Malcolm and Angus Young and Phil Rudd carrying on playing, what are they gonna call it? I mean they're not gonna call it 'We-Are-Not-AC/DC'. So you call it AC/DC, don't you?

I don't think they took too much flack, really. Of course, people will always say, 'Oh you can never replace Bon', but if Angus and Malcolm work together, what are they gonna call it? They just needed a singer. I don't think those sorts of decisions are easy to make, but it's AC/DC, isn't it? And I think they took

a long time over it, considering the future, but you know, you move on, and I think Bon would have liked his name, and his band, and his music, to be kept alive.

Yeah, I suppose they'd worked hard to get where they'd gotten to, hadn't they?
PW: Well, what does Angus do? Go off and form a folk band? They are a unit, they work together, so of course they're AC/DC. I think they did it with the greatest respect to Bon. They found the right singer with Brian, and my god, what a difficult job Brian had to do, you know?

What do you think their trademark sound was during those years? Is it particularly different to the later years with Brian?
PW: I think it was exactly the same really, just with a different singer! I mean, Brian added certain elements that are really good. The sound was something that everyone else wanted to copy, and it's very difficult to do.

Did you realise that they'd be headlining your shows by the end of the year?
PW: They didn't headline those shows. They did one or two shows where we split headlining things. It was after we'd stopped touring together that they went on and did their own shows. In fact, I believe they did California when we'd finished in the mid-west.

And do you think that's because they'd been such a success supporting you guys?
PW: Well, you certainly wouldn't put two bands that were capable of drawing ten or twelve thousand people together when you could make a lot more money having them play separately. At that point it was obvious that we didn't work together anymore. So AC/DC went on to do what AC/DC was desperate to do.

How do you rate those years, personally?

PW: Very good times, yeah. I mean, I enjoy myself when I'm playing so, yeah, very good times because you can capture a moment. I mean, I can tell you about countless times when UFO have played, where we've had a support band, special guests and all that. But imagine having AC/DC every night for several months...

And what about the rest of the British music scene? Do you think they really enjoyed having AC/DC around, because they played a lot in London, didn't they?

PW: Well, it's like having The Rolling Stones around, isn't it?

They fitted in alright, though? They were a completely different sound, weren't they?

PW: I think so. Well, I think they created it. I mean, what else have you got, I mean, I dunno, Caravan? I'm just knocking, you know...?

Were there any bands around at the time that tried to sound like them, or were they always unique?

PW: I think so many bands did try. It goes back to the college-type bands, doesn't it? Everybody wants to sound like that. Every guitar player thinks he's Angus at one point, but then, every singer wanted to sound like Robert Plant, didn't they? I mean, it's funny looking back - every singer wanted to sound like Robert Plant, but they didn't want to sound like Bon. They just wanted to live Bon's lifestyle.

As a last word on Bon, was he, for you, the archetypal rock 'n' roll front man?

PW: Yes he was. He got up in the morning, and he'd go straight to the bar and have a double Jack. I suppose so many people read about it and thought about it, but he did it. Sad, in a way, because it was his downfall in the end. Well that's... you know...?

That's rock and roll, man.

PW: Well, I suppose it is. I could tell you stuff about when we played Cleveland, Ohio with AC/DC as special guests - I know I keep saying special guests, but they were really special. Anyway, there was one time when Angus and Malcolm were having a fight backstage, arguing over whether to do 'Dirty Teacher' or another song as an encore. It was quite funny actually, them rolling around on the floor and then suddenly having to go onstage. And before you know it they're playing 'TNT', except you've just seen them rolling around having a fight.

Is that what they were like, just a couple of naughty brothers?

PW: I tell you something: they're very intelligent people, very intelligent. Very artistic and articulate - but I tell you what, they knew where their rock and roll came from and, without them, where would we be?

AC/DC: CHRONOLOGY

NOVEMBER, 1973 - Formed in Sydney by Scottish ex-pats, guitarist brothers Malcolm and Angus Young. This first line-up also featured Colin Burgess on drums, singer David Evans, with Larry Van Kreidt on bass and, at some gigs, saxophone.

DECEMBER, 1973 - The band adopt the moniker AC/DC after the Young's sister Margaret sees it written on a sewing machine.

FEBRUARY, 1974 - AC/DC's debut single 'Can I Sit Next To You?' is recorded in Sydney. Produced by George Young, the eldest Young brother and former member of the hugely popular Australian pop band The Easybeats, the single is released Australia-wide on the 'Albert' record label on the 22nd of July.

APRIL, 1974 - Angus Young wears his infamous school uniform on stage for the first time, again at the suggestion of his sister.

AUGUST, 1974 - AC/DC embark on a short Australian tour supporting Lou Reed and Stevie Wright, ex-lead singer of the The Easybeats. The same month they are introduced to Bon Scott, another Scottish-born Australian, through a mutual friend.

SEPTEMBER, 1974 - Dave Evans is fired after a gig in Melbourne, and Scott, the band's driver at the time, is brought in to replace him. Scott's first full gig is at the Brighton-le-sands Masonic hall in Sydney.

NOVEMBER, 1974 - The first AC/DC album, High Voltage, is recorded in an impressive ten days. George Young is joined at the helm by his Easybeats bandmate Harry Vanda. A session drummer is brought in for most of the recording, although

Peter Clack, the band's sometime drummer, contributes to one track, 'She's Got Balls'. The album is more glam rock than its successors, and even opens with a cover, 'Baby Please Don't Go', originally recorded by Big Joe Williams, a Delta Blues singer and guitarist. The band's love for early American blues is well-documented, Angus Young insisting in an interview from 2003 that the last record he bought was Muddy Waters' 1977 'comeback' Hard Rain.

FEBRUARY, 1975 - High Voltage is released in Australia, but initially fails to chart.

MARCH, 1975 - The band release a second single, 'Love Song (Oh Jene)', which was again unsuccessful at first. However, the B-side, their cover of 'Oh Baby Please Don't Go', is picked up by Australian radio and eventually reaches number ten on the national charts. By this time, the rhythm section had stabilised with the addition of Phil Rudd (drums) and Mark Evans (bass). This line-up would continue for the next two years; quite an achievement for a band so notoriously careless with bass players.

JUNE, 1975 - AC/DC's first headline gig at the festival hall in Melbourne, with Stevie Wright supporting (a reversed bill from the previous year). This was a landmark gig for the band, coinciding with their debut album going Gold in Australia.

JULY, 1975 - Flushed with domestic success, the band returned to the studio to record its second album, TNT. George Young and Harry Vanda once again oversaw the recording process, although this time there was no need for session musicians. The album spawned several songs that were to become set staples in the following years, including 'The Jack', the euphemistic tale of an especially promiscuous groupie with a particularly nasty affliction, and Bon's anthemic paean to the band's excessive, frenetic lifestyle, 'It's a Long Way To The Top (If You Wanna

Rock and Roll)'. The rest of the year was spent furiously touring Australia, stopping off on the way to record several appearances for national television.

DECEMBER, 1975 - On the 8th, 'It's A Long Way to The Top' was released as a single in Australia, and peaked at number five in the national charts. It was followed a week later by the TNT album, which was soon certified triple-gold. By the end of the month, AC/DC had cemented their status as Australia's top band by signing a worldwide record deal with Atlantic Records in London, home to Led Zeppelin, Yes and Foreigner, among others. The band celebrated a successful year with a New Year's Eve gig in Adelaide.

JANUARY, 1976 - The band, along with Vanda and Young, began sessions for what would become the band's third album, Dirty Deeds Done Dirt Cheap. The recording would become more protracted than their previous efforts, interrupted by the Australian single release of 'TNT', and the departure of the band to London at the end of March.

APRIL, 1976 - 'Its A Long Way To The Top' was finally released in the UK, backed with a Scott-fronted re-recording of their first Australian single, made for the TNT album and niftily re-titled, 'Can I Sit Next To You Girl'. The quintet caused a stir when they arrived in London, and immediately attracted a following due in part to an imagined association with the burgeoning punk-rock movement, presumably because of their particular no-frills brand of rock and roll, and their previous involvement with punk godfather Lou Reed.

MAY, 1976 - High Voltage is released in the UK, but fails to chart. The LP was actually a compilation of the band's first two Australian releases, featuring two tracks from the original High Voltage, 'Little Lover' and 'She's Got Balls'. The remaining seven songs were taken from TNT and included 'It's A Long

Way To The Top', 'The Jack' and, oddly enough, a track called 'High Voltage'.

JUNE, 1976 - The band recorded a session for legendary Radio 1 DJ John Peel, performing four tracks from the UK release of High Voltage, and no doubt helping to reinforce their punk credentials. June also saw their first headline show at the Marquee club in London, and their first full-scale UK tour.

NOVEMBER, 1976 - Dirty Deeds Done Dirt Cheap is released in the UK. The album was significantly different from the earlier Australian release, but once again it failed to chart. The album was rejected by Alantic in America, and not released until 1981. This delay, however, served the band and their record company well, since the record peaked at number three when it was eventually released.

DECEMBER, 1976 - After a year of touring the UK and Europe, including a date at the Reading festival with 40,000 onlookers, the band returned to their native Australia. Some dates, however, were cancelled by the Australian authorities,

who had become increasingly concerned by the scabrous reputation of the band.

JANUARY, 1977 - As was becoming the norm, the band began their year at Albert studios, this time working on their fourth album proper, Let There Be Rock. The relationship between Angus Young and Mark Evans became strained during these sessions, and the pressure of subsequent touring led to Evans' departure from AC/DC in May. Cliff Williams, his replacement, had previously played with Glaswegian singer-songwriter Al Stewart as well as with his own bands Bandit and Home, which had supported Led Zeppelin in 1971. The beginning of the year also saw the band's last Australian concerts before the tragic death of Bon Scott.

JUNE, 1977 - Let There Be Rock was released in the US, ahead of an extensive American tour that included dates with REO Speedwagon, Moxy and Styx, as well as headline shows of their own. The album eventually peaked at #154 on the billboard charts.

OCTOBER, 1977 - The LP was released in the UK, France and Germany, becoming the first AC/DC LP to chart in Britain, peaking at #17. The band embarked on a month-long tour of England, including a home-coming, of sorts, in Glasgow, before returning to the US for the remainder of the year.

APRIL, 1978 - April saw the recording of If You Want Blood (You've Got It), a live album taken mainly from the band's show at the Glasgow Apollo on the 30th of the month, notable for an encore performed while dressed in the Scottish football strip. The album's title inspired a song of the same name that later appeared on the following year's Highway To Hell.

MAY, 1978 - Powerage was released in the UK and the US. Whilst not as successful, commercially or critically, as Let There Be Rock, it is notable for being the last AC/DC album to have been produced by their long-time collaborators, George Young and Harry Vanda, before the duo's return to the producer's chair in 1986. The rest of the year was spent fulfilling an exhaustive touring schedule, culminating in two sold-out shows at the Hammersmith Odeon in London. If You Want Blood was released internationally at the end of the year while the band took a well-earned break from touring, letting their album do the leg-work.

FEBRUARY, 1979 - Under pressure from Atlantic, the band starts working on its next album in Miami. At the record company's suggestion, Led Zeppelin and Kiss producer Eddie Kramer oversaw these initial sessions. Kramer and the Youngs soon fell out of favour, however, and Kramer was sacked before a single track was completed and the sessions were aborted.

MARCH, 1979 - AC/DC started working with Robert "Mutt" Lange in London. This would be the start of a very fruitful relationship, producing three hugely successful albums, and leaving AC/DC as one of the biggest bands in the world. Lange had cut his teeth making radio-friendly records for British pop-punk bands City Boy and The Boomtown Rats, and he gave AC/DC the finely-honed sheen it needed to propel them further up the charts. The resulting album, Highway To Hell, was released in July and spawned two hit singles, 'Touch Too Much' and the title track. More touring followed; the band played 174 concerts throughout the year, mostly in the US, where the album had climbed to #17 on the Billboard charts, and was certified Gold after just three months of release.

FEBRUARY, 1980 - The year had started well for the band with another spate of concerts in France and the UK, the last being at Southampton's Gaumont theatre on the 27th of January. On the 7th of February, AC/DC played 'Touch Too Much' on Top Of The Pops, their last time on the programme with Scott. After spending the night of the 18th of February drinking with friends in London, Scott was found in his car the next day, having choked on his own vomit.

MARCH, 1980 - Despite the tragedy, the band decided that Scott would have wanted them to press on with the new album, and so began to audition possible replacements. Ex-Geordie singer Brian Johnson was selected from a shortlist that reportedly included Easybeats singer Stevie Wright, Gary Holton (who would later go on to star in Auf Weidersehen, Pet, an ITV drama that revolved around the lives of seven British construction workers), Aussie Alan Fryer and Terry Schlesser, who went on to replace Johnson in Geordie.

APRIL, 1980 - Back In Black was recorded in the Bahamas, again with Mutt Lange at the helm. The album was released in July and climbed to the top of the UK album chart. An international tour followed, cementing Johnson's role as the new AC/DC singer and confirming the band's position as one of the most popular rock bands in the world.

FEBRUARY, 1981 - February saw the band return to its homeland for the first time since the beginning of 1977. They played five dates across Australia and were rapturously received wherever they went.

JULY, 1981 - For Those About To Rock (We Salute You), the band's second record with Johnson and third with Lange, is recorded in Paris. In August, the band took a break from recording to headline the second annual Monsters Of Rock festival at Castle Donington in the UK. The bill also featured the likes of Whitesnake, Slade and Blue Oyster Cult. The Aussie band would later go on to headline the festival twice more (in 1984 and 1991), a record for Donington. The album was released in November, becoming their first US number 1.

DECEMBER, 1981 - The band's new-found superstardom in the US attracted undue attention in the shape of legal action, brought forward by a couple in Chicago who claimed they had been receiving obscene phone calls at their home number of 362 436; the number mentioned in 'Dirty Deeds Done Dirt Cheap', which had eventually received its stateside release earlier in the year - ('Call me any time/Just Dial 36-24-36/I Lead A Life Of Crime').

JANUARY, 1982 - The year started badly for AC/DC, as they lost out to Anglo-Aussie balladeers Air Supply at the American Music Awards, where they were up for Best Rock Band. The rest of 1982 was mixed for the band – they continued touring, first America, then Japan (their last visit), then the UK – but they were forced to cancel a tour of mainland Europe.

MARCH, 1983 - March saw rehearsals begin in earnest for Flick Of The Switch, the quintet's ninth studio album. The self-produced record was initiated in April, with some help from AC/DC's original production team, Harry Vanda and George Young, under the name 'The Gorgeous Glaswegian'. Phil Rudd, whose alcohol problems were proving too much for the other band members, was asked to leave during the sessions for the album. He was replaced by Simon Wright, who also appeared in the two promotional videos made by the band shortly after the album's completion. Flick Of The Switch, released in August, reached number 4 in the UK, and was another considerable success for the band.

OCTOBER, 1983 The band embarked on a three-month US tour, including a short diversion to Canada. They ended the year on a high, playing to a capacity crowd at New York's Madison Square Garden on the 19th of December.

JANUARY, 1984 - FEBRUARY, 1985 - Rehearsing and recording for Fly On The Wall, studio album number ten, took thirteen months, interspersed with several months of touring, including a 'Monsters Of Rock' tour in the August of 1984. The album, released in July, was the band's first to be released on CD. It fared well in the UK, this time peaking at number 7.

OCTOBER, 1985 - AC/DC found themselves at the centre of a media circus following 'revelations' that serial killer Richard Ramirez was a fan, and in fact inspired by the band's 1979 track 'Nightprowler', a song which features references to the sitcom and Robin Williams' vehicle, 'Mork and Mindy'. The American press, infuriated by the discovery of an AC/DC baseball cap at the crime scene, immediately branded the band Satanists.

DECEMBER, 1985 - AC/DC reconvened at Compass Point studios in the Bahamas, this time with Vanda and Young producing. The band emerged with one song, 'Who Made Who?', and two instrumentals, 'D.T.' and 'Chase The Ace'. The first was released as a single the following May, while all three are included on the Who Made Who album.

MAY, 1986 - Who Made Who was released. The album was the soundtrack to Stephen King's first (and only) directorial effort, an adaptation of his short story 'Trucks'. All three tracks from December's recording session were included alongside some choice cuts from Johnson's stint as vocalist, as well as 'Ride On', from 1976's Dirty Deeds Done Dirt Cheap, featuring Bon Scott. The LP reached number 11 in the UK, while its title track peaked at number sixteen in the singles chart. The film, however, did not fare so well, with King declaring it a "moron movie" and retiring from directing soon after.

AUGUST, 1987 - AC/DC began work on the follow-up, titled Blow Up Your Video. The band retained its trusty production team of Vanda and Young, producing nineteen tracks in eleven fruitful days. Later in the year, tickets for the band's February tour of Australia were put on sale. Sixty-three people were arrested in the clamour for tickets.

JANUARY, 1988 - 'Heatseeker' was released in the UK, climbing to number 12 in the chart, and becoming AC/DC's quickest ever selling single in the process. The album followed a month later, hailed by many as a return to form. It reached number two in Britain, and number twelve in America. The band spent the whole year playing arenas in support of the album, starting off in Australia in February (their first tour there in seven years), and ending the year in America.

NOVEMBER, 1989 - Simon Wright left the band to play with Ex-Rainbow and Black Sabbath vocalist Ronnie James Dio. Chris Slade was brought in, on a temporary basis at first, to take over drumming duties while the band rehearsed new material.

OCTOBER, 1990 - The Razor's Edge, AC/DC's thirteenth studio album, was released worldwide. The album climbed to number two on the US Billboard, and number four in the

UK. The band embarked on a huge world tour shortly after the album's release.

JANUARY, 1991 - The year began on a tragic note after three fans were crushed to death during the band's show in Salt Lake City. The band pressed on, however, and played 143 dates by the end of the year, including a third headline performance at the 'Monsters Of Rock' festival. On the 28th of September, AC/DC headline the 'Rock Around The Bloc' festival in Moscow, only a month after an attempted coup (the 'August Pustch') by conservative Soviets. The free concert, attended by nearly 1,000,000 Russians, passed without incident.

JANUARY, 1992 - The majority of the year was spent selecting tracks for a forthcoming live album, using recordings of various shows from the '90/'91 tour, including Castle Donington. Live, mixed (and reportedly "re-touched") by producer Bruce Fairbarn, who had worked with the band on Razor's Edge, was released in Europe on the 29th of October and reached number five in the chart.

JUNE, 1993 - The single 'Big Gun', backed by a previously unreleased live version of 'Back In Black' from 1991's Moscow show, was released in the UK and reached number twenty-three in the UK. The track was produced by Rick Rubin, who had previously worked with the Beastie Boys and the Red Hot Chili Peppers to widespread acclaim. The song was used on the soundtrack to Arnold Schwarzenegger's latest blockbuster, Last Action Hero, an action-film parody from Die Hard director John Mctiernan. Indeed, Schwarzenegger featured in the David Mallet-directed video, dressed in Angus's trademark school uniform.

JUNE, 1994 - The band began work on its next album, with Rubin in the producer's chair. Phil Rudd rejoined the band after kicking his drinking habit. Between July and September,

Atlantic reissued nine digitally remastered AC/DC albums, from the 1976 version of High Voltage to 1983's Flick Of The Switch.

SEPTEMBER, 1995 - Ballbreaker was released throughout Europe and the US. It charted strongly on both sides of the Atlantic, reaching number six in the UK and number four in America.

JANUARY, 1996 - The band spent most of the year touring the world, including their native Australia. 1996 also saw them film their appearance for shock-jock Howard Stern's 1997 autobiopic Private Parts, based on his book of the same name. AC/DC also filmed an intimate show for VH1 in London that included some rarely heard Bon Scott-era numbers, including 'Riff-Raff' from 1978's Powerage.

NOVEMBER, 1997 - The Bonfire box-set was released in the US. A five-disc set, it featured a 1977 recording of the band live from Atlantic studios in New York; the soundtrack to the concert film Let There Be Rock filmed on 9th of December 1979 spread over two discs; a collection of rare Bon Scott tracks entitled Volts and a remastered edition of Back In Black. The band signed with EMI in the UK in December, and Bonfire was released there later the same month. The band's new record company re-issued Highway To Hell, For Those About To Rock, Fly On The Wall and Flick Of The Switch in January, followed by the other albums later in the year.

AUGUST, 1998 - The band received a lifetime achievement award from Kerrang! magazine, a UK publication that began life as a one-off supplement in Sounds magazine dedicated to the New Wave Of British Heavy Metal, a movement of which AC/DC are considered forefathers. The rest of the year was spent writing the follow up to Ballbreaker.

JULY, 1999 - The band relocated to Vancouver to start work on their sixteenth studio effort. The Young's older brother George was again producing, just as he did twenty-five years earlier.

FEBRUARY, 2000 - Stiff Upper Lip was released, reaching number twelve in the UK and number seven in the US. The subsequent world tour, beginning in August, took in 17 countries and 139 shows, ending on the 8th of July 2001 in Köln. The set-list was packed with classics, but by the end of the tour it only included one song from the band's most recent album. The end of 2001 saw Brian Johnson re-join Geordie for a small pub and club tour in the north of England, including a show at Newcastle's Opera House.

APRIL, 2002 - Brian Johnson, along with actor Brendan Healey, wrote a musical entitled Helen Of Troy.

MARCH, 2003 - The band was inducted into the rock and roll hall of fame, after being nominated for three years running. July saw the band support the Rolling Stones over three dates in June. October also saw the band returning to the legendary Hammersmith Odeon.

MAY, 2006 - Reports appeared in the Sydney Morning Herald that AC/DC had written their follow up to Stiff Upper Lip, but as yet had no definite recording plans. Johnson was believed to be handling the lyric-writing for the first time since 1988, and it was rumoured that the band had written enough material for a double album. In December 2006, the Daily Mirror reported that the band had been asked to headline a concert at Slane Castle in Ireland, possibly in the summer of 2007.

AC/DC: THE RECORDINGS

ALL SUMMARIES and comments are based on the original Australasian and UK releases. References are included for US releases where they differ from the originals. Single releases have been omitted as there were just too damn many!

It should be noted that most of the UK and US releases have been recently re-packaged in digi-pack form. There are no bonus tracks which really is a shame but the presentation is good all the same. All have nice artwork with original covers and (usually) informative notes. The notes covering the Bon Scott years and early Brian Johnson era are far more informative (and in most cases better written) than the albums covering the mid eighties onwards. Well worth picking up for the collection anyway.

AC/DC – Loud! So loud! Solid, highly predictable and ever so much fun if you ever got the chance to see them live. AC/DC are a rock and roll band (no, not metal!) that are revered by millions and no doubt hated by just as many. Australia's AC/DC are probably only one of two bands in the history of rock and roll that have stuck so consistently to their guns with respect of their music despite what critics and other odd-bods the world over have said to try and get them to change direction. With the recent release of their thirty-third album (no I couldn't believe it either) Status Quo are certainly the other. With the Quo becoming an institution of British Rock and Roll the two bands in some ways are very similar. Both have become entertainment icons in their respective countries and both have delivered album after album, that let's face it are pretty much in the same vein from start to finish. Although AC/DC have not (yet) delivered thirty three albums (AC/DC are nearing twenty excluding live packages) They have certainly become a highly recognisable feature on the rock and roll landscape.

Both bands however have a knack of usually delivering solid and fun albums to play. This and their ability to deliver absolutely top-class live shows (in the case of AC/DC) almost every time have made them winners.

Where they have differed as far as the record industry is concerned is in AC/DC's huge success in the North American market. AC/DC last year were the fifth biggest selling recording artist in America. One album alone, Back In Black has exceeded forty million albums sales the world over.

HIGH VOLTAGE

Original Australian release. Alberts.
Released 17th February 1975.
Produced by Harry Vanda and George Young.

Recorded in Sydney in November 1974 between gigs over a ten day period this more than acceptable debut album release wasn't going to catapult the band to immediate fame and fortune. It did however set them well on their way as far as recording was concerned. It's rather baffling however given the interest AC/DC has commanded over the years why the original debut album has never been re-mastered. It can be obtained as an Australian and New Zealand import.

For the real collector there are also some interesting facsimile copies that have emerged from former East Bloc countries.

Although this was the album debut the band (minus Bon) had laid down a single called Can I Sit Next To You Girl?, and this was backed by Rockin' In The Parlour, both were sung by the original singer Dave Evans whom Bon replaced in short order just prior to the recording of the debut album High Voltage in late 1974.

Shortly after the recording of the debut album founder member Rob Bailey who was the band's bass player on the album was given the axe. He was replaced by Mark Evans.

The album overall is a good one and it is well worth trying to hunt down this original Australasian release as it is a far better listen, especially in historical terms than the re-hashed compilation issued a few years later.

BABY PLEASE DON'T GO *(Joe Williams)*

The track was not released outside of Australia until it was included on the 1984 release of '74 Jailbreak. Ten years after the original High Voltage release. This is a song that is baffling to see why it was omitted from the 'foreign' releases. A classic Big Joe Williams number this had actually been covered with great success by Welsh rockers Budgie only two years earlier. After hearing this version it is easy to hear the obvious similarities in the execution of the song. Classic song recorded by a classic band and even today both the AC/DC and Budgie versions stand out amongst the best ever (rather numerous) covers of this song. Interestingly the song was released as a single in Australia and after much radio (and TV) airplay it reached number ten in the national charts. With this in mind it is even more baffling why it was omitted from the foreign release of High Voltage!

SHE'S GOT BALLS *(A Young/M Young/B Scott)*

This track was later included on the 'overseas' version of High Voltage over two years after the original High Voltage release. A version was also released on the Bonfire box set on the Volts disc. This, however, was a live rendition. Not a bad song considering it was one of their first efforts.

LITTLE LOVER *(A Young/M Young/B Scott)*

This track was later included on the 'overseas' version of High Voltage over two years after the original High Voltage release.

Little blues number and for AC/DC a rather mundane one. Not the highlight of Bon's singing career!

STICK AROUND *(A Young/M Young/B Scott)*

This track was not included on the 'overseas' version of High Voltage or any other compilation to date. Not a bad number and it's a shame that the original debut album from AC/DC has not been given the re-master and digi-pack treatment that most other albums have. The success of AC/DC certainly justifies its reissue.

SOUL STRIPPER *(B Scott/M Young)*

The track was not released outside of Australia until it was included on the 1984 release of '74 Jailbreak ten years afters the original High Voltage release. Why this song was left off the non Australasian album is quite baffling as the song really does have a great grove. Simple and ever so derivative but a great listen (turn that volume right up!) all the same. Simple but effective guitar solo in this one with great rhythm punching in behind. It displayed all the things AC/DC were to exude for many years hence.

YOU AIN'T GOT A HOLD ON ME *(A Young/M Young/B Scott)*

The track was not released outside of Australia until it was included on the 1984 release of '74 Jailbreak ten years afters the original High Voltage release. This song was omitted from the UK and US versions of the High Voltage album.

The start of this song sounds almost exactly like something Free might have recorded. That is testament in itself that this was a band on their way. The guitar sound it so much like Paul Kossoff it's spooky. The album is worth it for this song alone! Although the song itself is not an absolute killer the sounds the band are squeezing out of the guitars are top notch.

LOVE SONG *(A Young/M Young/B Scott)*

This track was not included on the 'overseas' version of High

Voltage or any other compilation to date. Although this is album filler it's still good considering it was on a band's debut. It would be nice to see this get a proper reissue as well.

SHOW BUSINESS *(A Young/M Young/B Scott)*
The track was not released outside of Australia until it was included on the 1984 release of '74 Jailbreak ten years after the original High Voltage release. The song delivers a similar message and is a precursor to It's A Long Way To The Top (If You Wanna Rock 'n' Roll) from the band's follow up (in Oz) album T.N.T.

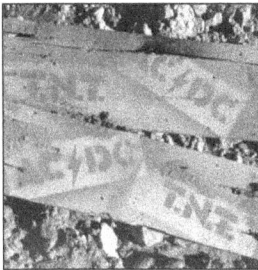

T.N.T

Original Australian release. Alberts.
Released December 1975.
Produced by Harry Vanda and George Young.

After recording their debut album High Voltage in late 1974 and rushing it out on the streets in February it was quite a feat for the band to record another piece of product so quickly. The band had undergone some line-up changes and it was for this album that messrs. Young, Young, Scott, Evans and Rudd started their relationship. This was to last until after the recording of Let There Be Rock when Evans departed and was replaced by Englishman Cliff Williams.

Again it's rather baffling however given the interest AC/DC has commanded over the years why the original sophomore album has never been re-mastered either. It's certainly one of the best albums from the line-ups featuring Bon Scott and it retains a sparseness that works extremely well. AC/DC were unable to capture that sound for a long time after its release and it remains one of the more interesting albums from the period because of its simplicity. It can be obtained (a non-re-mastered CD version) as an Australian and New Zealand import. Once again for the real collector there are also some interesting facsimile copies (of extremely good quality sound and artwork) that have emerged from former East Bloc countries.

As a second album this was a vast improvement on the more than acceptable debut and is again an album that is well worth hunting down in its original T.N.T. form. The album, raw as it is, still rates as one of the best AC/DC albums ever.

IT'S A LONG WAY TO THE TOP
(IF YOU WANNA ROCK 'N' ROLL)
(A Young/M Young/B Scott)
Still one of the best (and most memorable) songs AC/DC ever recorded and released. This was issued as a single in Australasia and it even had a video (yes, more than five years before the real advent of MTV!) A simple riffing rocker that makes extremely good use of bagpipes. Classic AC/DC at a very early stage.
This track was later included on the 'overseas' version of High Voltage over a year after T.N.T.'s release.

ROCK 'N' ROLL SINGER *(A Young/M Young/B Scott)*
Fairly straight forward rocker that really shines because of Bon's social commentary on a rock and roll singer's duties in life. The song certainly caused consternation in some schools down-under with the use of the word shit. Well, it was 1975 you know! This track was later included on the 'overseas' version of High Voltage over a year after T.N.T.'s release.

THE JACK *(A Young/M Young/B Scott)*
Another track that was to become a classic. Live this really came into its own, especially with Bon's rather filthy anecdotes at times. Simple but extremely effective guitar solo from Angus. This track was later included on the 'overseas' version of High Voltage over a year after T.N.T.'s release.

LIVE WIRE *(A Young/M Young/B Scott)*
With the simplest start known to (Neanderthal) man this track,

amateurish as it may have been, actually worked quite well. Certainly a track that could give Status Quo a run for their money! Two chord what? Bon's little comment of 'stick this in your fuse box' is classic. This track was later included on the 'overseas' version of High Voltage over a year after T.N.T.'s release.

T.N.T. *(A Young/M Young/B Scott)*

Simplicity ruled with this album that was for sure but then that was the secret to AC/DC's success. Tight but simple riffs layered with guitar and a simple but tough rhythm section ploughing away beneath. Add Bon Scott's raucous vocal and straight to the point lyrics and what do you have? T.N.T. is a perfect example. Simple tough rock and roll by numbers. This track was later included on the 'overseas' version of High Voltage over a year after T.N.T.'s release.

ROCKER *(A Young/M Young/B Scott)*

Just when you thought it might calm down the Rocking really starts up. All the clichés are here but what the hell it sounds good! This is another example of how Bon and the boys could pull off a coup with ever so simple numbers. They had a sound! This is one track that was not picked for the 'overseas' version of High Voltage but instead made its appearance later on the 'overseas' version of Dirty Deeds Done Dirt Cheap which was released in 1981.

CAN I SIT NEXT TO YOU GIRL *(A Young/M Young)*

Originally recorded by the very first version of AC/DC (with Dave Evans on vocals) It is a simple song that has been slated by many a journalist over the years (maybe they were all gay and just didn't understand what this simple song was all about!) Yes it's simple, even a little bit naff but how can one resist that gritty vocal from Bon. Another track that is cliché ridden but it works very, very well. Lyrics not penned by Bon as he was not in the band at the time of writing. This track was later included on the 'overseas' version of High Voltage over a year after T.N.T.'s release. The original version with Dave Evans was backed by another as yet unreleased track called Rockin' In The Parlour and to this day these remain unreleased.

HIGH VOLTAGE *(A Young/M Young/B Scott)*
Title track of the band's debut release it was actually included on their second album! Simple but effective this quickly became a popular live track. This track was later included on the 'overseas' version of High Voltage over a year after T.N.T.'s release.

SCHOOL DAYS *(C Berry)*
Listen to a lot (well most!) of AC/DC's early work (especially their live gigs) and you can certainly hear the influence of Chuck Berry and to some extent Bo Diddley on the playing, the guitar playing in particular. Angus and Malcolm Young's guitar interplay apparent even at this early stage and Bon's gritty vocals starting to define a sound that if nothing else was original. This is the second track off this release that was not included on the later 'overseas' compilation of High Voltage.

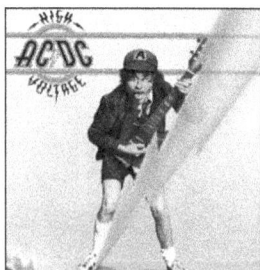

HIGH VOLTAGE

Overseas version.
Originally released as Atco 36-142.
Released 28th September 1976.
Produced by Harry Vanda and George Young.

Released over eighteen months after the original High Voltage (which was the band's real debut released in February 1975) this 'overseas' version holds little resemblance to its earlier namesake. Instead most of the tracks were lifted from AC/DC's (original) follow up album T.N.T. which had been released in Australia and New Zealand in December 1975.

The songs of course are great but nothing really beats the original release with the hitherto unreleased tracks. The Atlantic release of High Voltage in the US and the UK is known to the uninitiated as their debut. Good as the album is, it is not their debut. Far from it in fact. You have been warned! It is in fact the equivalent of their second and half album!

IT'S A LONG WAY TO THE TOP
(IF YOU WANNA ROCK 'N' ROLL)
(A Young/M Young/B Scott)

Originally released on the Australasian only release T.N.T. in 1975. Still one of the best (and most memorable) songs AC/DC ever recorded and released. This was issued as a single in Australasia and it even had a video (yes, more than five years before the real advent of MTV!) A simple riffing rocker that makes extremely good use of bagpipes. Classic AC/DC at a very early stage.

ROCK 'N' ROLL SINGER *(A Young/M Young/B Scott)*

Originally released on the Australasian only release T.N.T. in 1975. Fairly straight forward rocker that really shines because of Bon's social commentary on a rock and roll singer's duties in life. The song certainly caused consternation in some schools down-under with the use of the word shit. Well, it was 1975 you know!

THE JACK *(A Young/M Young/B Scott)*

Originally released on the Australasian only release T.N.T. in 1975. Another track that was to become a classic. Live this really came into its own, especially with Bon's rather filthy anecdotes at times. Simple but extremely effective guitar solo from Angus.

LIVE WIRE *(A Young/M Young/B Scott)*

Originally released on the Australasian only release T.N.T. in

1975. With the simplest start known to (Neanderthal) man this track, amateurish as it may have been, actually worked quite well. Certainly a track that could give Status Quo a run for their money! Two chord what? Bon's little comment of 'stick this in your fuse-box' is classic.

T.N.T. *(A Young/M Young/B Scott)*
Originally released on the Australasian only release T.N.T. in 1975. Simplicity ruled with this album that was for sure but then that was the secret to AC/DC's success. Tight but simple riffs layered with guitar and a simple but tough rhythm section ploughing away beneath. Add Bon Scott's raucous vocal and straight to the point lyrics and what do you have? T.N.T. is a perfect example. Simple tough rock and roll by numbers.

CAN I SIT NEXT TO YOU GIRL *(B Scott/M Young)*
Originally released on the Australasian only release T.N.T. in 1975. Simple song that has been slated by many a journalist over the years (maybe they were all gay and just didn't understand what this simple song was all about!) Yes it's simple, even a little bit naff but how can one resist that gritty vocal from Bon. Another track that is cliché ridden but it works very, very well. Interestingly lyrics not penned by Bon. The original version with Dave Evans was backed by another as yet unreleased track called Rockin' In The Parlour.

LITTLE LOVER *(A Young/M Young/B Scott)*
Originally released on the Australasian debut release entitled High Voltage which was released in early 1975. Little blues number and for AC/DC a rather mundane one. Not the highlight of Bon's singing career!

SHE'S GOT BALLS *(A Young/M Young/B Scott)*
Originally released on the Australasian debut release entitled High Voltage in early 1975. Was also released on the Bonfire box set on the Volts disc. This however was a live rendition.

Not a bad song considering it was one of their first efforts.

HIGH VOLTAGE *(A Young/M Young/B Scott)*
Originally released on the Australasian only release T.N.T. in 1975. Title track of the band's debut release it was actually included on their second album! Simple but effective this quickly became a popular live track.

NB: It should be noted that there were several different sets of cover art for High Voltage over various releases world-wide.

DIRTY DEEDS DONE DIRT CHEAP

Original Australian release. Alberts.
Released September 1976.
Produced by Harry Vanda and George Young.

In Australia and New Zealand this was the third studio album that had been delivered by AC/DC and the band was becoming increasingly popular on the live circuit. A revised version (and not for the better I might add) was setup for release in the UK, US and other parts of the globe. As it happens the album was not released in the US until 1981.

The version listed here is the Australasian release and not only did it have a far better track listing it also had a much better cover. Still, the fingers in the air from Angus may well have been too much for the Americans to deal with in 1976. In New Zealand this third album was lapped up by the (few) hard rockers the land possessed. In Australia the band were becoming more and more popular so it was essential for them to deliver more product. Once again for the real collector there are also some interesting facsimile copies (of extremely good quality sound and artwork) that have emerged of this release from former East Bloc countries.

DIRTY DEEDS DONE DIRT CHEAP
(A Young/M Young/B Scott)

Classic lyrics by Bon and this album was up and running. The song is a mini anthem in its own right and the song soon became very popular on the live circuit. This track was included on the 'overseas' release of Dirty Deeds.

AIN'T NO FUN (WAITING AROUND TO BE A MILLIONAIRE) *(A Young/M Young/B Scott)*

Although this is a very basic rock and roll number with quite a slow groove it is actually one of the better tracks on the album. Bon's little story of rags to riches (or at least waiting around for it to happen) is quite entertaining. The song was lifted from this original release and included on the US and UK versions of Dirty Deeds.

THERE'S GONNA BE SOME ROCKIN'
(A Young/M Young/B Scott)

A simple rock and roll number. Good little sing-along number but really it's just good album filler. The song was lifted from the Australasian version and included on Dirty Deeds in the UK (1976) and the US (1981).

PROBLEM CHILD *(A Young/M Young/B Scott)*

Another Bon Scott anthem this was also to become a much requested live number. With rock solid (excuse the pun!) riffs from the guitar maestros Problem Child has remained a live favourite to date. Bon's interpretation has really never been bettered however. This version was lifted and included on the 1981 'overseas' version of Dirty Deeds. A slightly different (and shorter) version of Problem Child was included on 1977's Let There Be Rock in place of Crabsody In Blue in some territories. This was another one of those rather bizarre record company executive decisions!

SQUEALER *(A Young/M Young/B Scott)*

A good plodding rocker to end this version of the album on. Fantastic guitar playing in this one and well worth giving it a good listen at full volume. This was lifted from the original 1976 release and included on the 'overseas' versions of Dirty Deeds.

BIG BALLS *(A Young/M Young/B Scott)*

As near as AC/DC ever got to singing cabaret! With Bon's dirty lyrics this one was certainly an amusing addition. Quite an entertaining number all in all. This track was included on the 'overseas' release of Dirty Deeds.

R.I.P. (ROCK IN PEACE) *(A Young/M Young/B Scott)*

Why this was not included on the overseas versions is anyone's guess. Another quaint number that only Bon could have penned.

RIDE ON *(A Young/M Young/B Scott)*

Along with Jailbreak this is easily the best of the bunch on this album. Almost as good as AC/DC ever got with true blues. Lifted from this original Dirty Deeds release it was included on the 'overseas' versions. The song was also used on the Stephen King movie Maximum Overdrive as part of the soundtrack. It was also included on the Who Made Who album which AC/DC issued in lieu of the full soundtrack.

JAILBREAK *(A Young/M Young/B Scott)*

Also released as a single in the UK (with a still unreleased B-side, Fling Thing) Jailbreak should have been a huge hit and although it did make it in some rather far flung territories like Brazil it did not have the impact it deserved. In the UK the single may well have not hit its intended target because of Thin Lizzy's monster album of that year called Jailbreak. A stage favourite with Bon Scott on vocals it is one of the better earlier tracks sung by Brian Johnson. If one had to make a choice to take one AC/DC song to a desert island this would certainly be my choice cut.

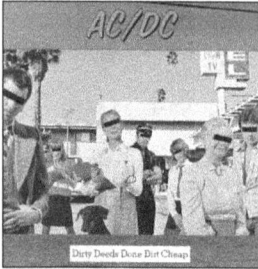

DIRTY DEEDS DONE DIRT CHEAP

Overseas version. Atco 16033.
Released 27th March 1981.
Produced by Harry Vanda and George Young.

Why the original Dirty Deeds was not released in the US in 1976 when it first made its appearance is anyone's guess (no doubt a rather foolish record company exec!) As for it's appearance (and rather altered state!) in 1981... well that one is obvious... AC/DC had become one of the biggest selling rock bands on the planet and the US market was hungry for more product.

It was a bit of a no-brainer for a group of record company execs to figure previously unreleased (in the US) product would sell. This version is the one the majority of people know but it is certainly not the best version. For the omission of Jailbreak on the US version alone one should question the individual's musical judgement who made the compilation decisions at the time. The song is a classic and it is worth locating the original release for that alone. So popular were AC/DC that this re-issued version of the album still sold by the truckload and it is nice to have this as a re-mastered digi-pack version. The additional tracks are listed below.

LOVE AT FIRST FEEL *(A Young/M Young/B Scott)*
Another classic dirty ditty, albeit a rather heavy one with Bon's clever double edged lyrics. This was not included on the original Dirty Deeds release from 1976 although the track was recorded in 1976.

ROCKER *(A Young/M Young/B Scott)*
Originally released on the band's second album T.N.T. it did not make an appearance until 1976 outside of Australasia.

All the clichés are here but what the hell it sounds good! This is another example of how Bon and the boys could pull off a coup with ever so simple numbers. They had a sound!

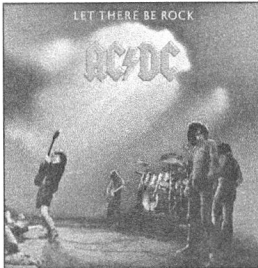

LET THERE BE ROCK

Originally released as Atco 36151.
Released 23rd June 1977.
Produced by Harry Vanda and George Young.

This is the album where AC/DC's sound started to sound reasonably cohesive rather than just a collection of good but often unrelated songs. Bon's lyric writing was certainly becoming less brash and the riffing Young brothers were becoming highly adept at writing killer guitar parts. Let There Be Rock was also the last album to feature Mark Evans on bass. He was to be replaced by Englishman Cliff Williams for the next studio effort, Powerage. Let There Be Rock however is still a great one to listen to with the volume knob twisted around past ten of course! Interestingly, it was a release that featured one cover for the Australian market and another for the rest of the world.

GO DOWN *(A Young/M Young/B Scott)*
A good solid start to the album that showed real progression. The track isn't really anything special but it works all the same. A thumping start to an album that wasn't going to let up from start to finish.

DOG EAT DOG *(A Young/M Young/B Scott)*
With a classic presentation of Bon's whining vocals this one for some reason really works. Off-beat drums and a classic AC/DC bass line the rhythm section really goes for it on this number. The guitar solo although barely covering two notes really works well. This is a perfect example of how AC/DC could pull off a great performance on so few (different) notes.

LET THERE BE ROCK *(A Young/M Young/B Scott)*

If there was ever a song that defined AC/DC during the Bon Scott years then this must be it. Classic fast riff as an intro from the Young brothers then a fine entrance with rollicking bass and thumpingly simple drums, Bon starts his sermon on rock and roll. A simple (but highly innovative) idea the lyrical content is nothing short of brilliant. This must surely be one of the finest anthems to rock and roll ever written and recorded. There is not a bad note in the whole song. Bon really lets rip with his vocals and whenever the singing ends a verse the guitar solos obliterate everything else. A great song on it's own it is absolutely perfect when played along with the video, and everyone should own the video to Let There Be Rock. Class stuff.

BAD BOY BOOGIE *(A Young/M Young/B Scott)*

Another bone crunching tune executed with simple perfection by AC/DC. This became a highly popular live number and was even issued on AC/DC's first official live album If You Want Blood You've Got It.

PROBLEM CHILD *(A Young/M Young/B Scott)*

Another Bon Scott anthem this was also to become a much requested live number. With rock solid (excuse the pun!) riffs from the guitar maestros Problem Child has remained a live favourite to date. Bon's interpretation has really never been bettered however.

OVERDOSE *(A Young/M Young/B Scott)*

Nice slow chords from the Youngs. A sound that was actually to become more prevalent after Bon's death Overdose really does just what is says as far as riffs are concerned in the song. The song has some rather understated (but brilliant) guitar soloing in the centre section and the riff is as solid as anything AC/DC had delivered to date and the song quite frankly should have been a lot more popular than it appeared to be.

HELL AIN'T A BAD PLACE TO BE *(A Young/M Young/B Scott)*
Another tough number delivered in a way that only AC/DC could. Classically simple Hell Ain't A Bad Place To Be is a song that once played it sticks in your brain for a very long time! The song, although very good as a studio track really shone when Bon Scott delivered this live. Once again a song that makes almost any listener want to pick an air guitar and go wild.

WHOLE LOTTA ROSIE *(A Young/M Young/B Scott)*
One of the most enduring AC/DC songs and certainly one of the most popular. Funny lyrics for any guy who has ever got The Fat Lady to Sing! .... Bon delivered this one ever so well. The track actually started (and was laid down to tape) as Dirty Eyes which was later released on the Volts CD in the Bonfire Box set. It is interesting to hear the development of the track from this initial recording to what became Whole Lotta Rosie. Great end to a thoroughly enjoyable album.

NB: On the Australasian version of Let There Be Rock the album featured a rather cool blues based track called Crabsody In Blue. On other versions this was replaced with Problem Child. One wonders a little about the rather benign lyrics however and maybe that's why the Americans dropped it. The track did however seem more in place on the album than Problem Child.

POWERAGE

Originally released as Atco 19180.
Released on 30th May 1978 as Atco 16033.
Produced by Harry Vanda and George Young.

Powerage was the debut album for English bassist Cliff Williams after the departure of Mark Evans and although the addition was not openly apparent to the casual listener Williams certainly brought a cohesiveness to the playing that had sometimes

been absent on previous studio recordings. Powerage was also the last Bon Scott era recording to be produced by Harry Vanda and George Young. The album is a really good one to listen to nearly thirty years on and quite frankly the one negative feature about the album is the rather dated cover. Still if you like Angus pulling faces...

ROCK 'N' ROLL DAMNATION *(A Young/M Young/B Scott)*
This is great start to a more than acceptable album. The song has everything that is good about AC/DC in it and it even features girl singers and maracas in the middle section. This is certainly one of the best tracks Vanda and Young ever produced for AC/DC. Also a very popular track live.

DOWN PAYMENT BLUES *(A Young/M Young/B Scott)*
Second track in and the album so far doesn't falter as far as the rockin' stakes are concerned. A tough down and dirty little number that Bon sings to perfection. Certainly one of the best tracks on the album.

GIMME A BULLET *(A Young/M Young/B Scott)*
A 'romantic' song from one of Bon's run-ins with ladies-a-waiting. Good rollicking rock and roll.

RIFF RAFF *(A Young/M Young/B Scott)*
A song that was to become a live classic for the band and quite rightly so. This was nothing less than balls to the wall rock and roll with fantastic frenetic guitar playing. Bon's desperate vocals really give this song an urgent feel. Another track that is perfect for the air guitar brigade.

SIN CITY *(A Young/M Young/B Scott)*
Another live favourite, this time a song with a slouching sleazy groove that is very much driven by Phil Rudd's drumming. Cool lyrics that will give a whole new meaning to Snakes and Ladders and living rich.

WHAT'S NEXT TO THE MOON *(A Young/M Young/B Scott)*

Also known as Next To The Moon and although not as well known as Sin City or Riff Raff this is another slow grooving rocker all the same. Simple but cool bass playing sets this one apart with it's intermix of simple but classy rhythm playing. Unusual in its use of backing vocals by at least three members of the band.

GONE SHOOTIN' *(A Young/M Young/B Scott)*

Not that there is a really weak spot on this album, this track however does seem to lack the killer instinct of the six previous tracks. It's rock and roll given the Acker-dacker treatment all the same. Listen to it on headphones (or your head between the speakers and you will hear that good old sixties production trick (effect!) of flipping from channel to channel. Someone had obviously been smoking a few spliffs while this one was laid down!... probably in the engineer's booth.

UP TO MY NECK IN YOU *(A Young/M Young/B Scott)*

Another fairly straight forward rocker from the masters of rockers! Nice guitar solos too.

KICKED IN THE TEETH *(A Young/M Young/B Scott)*

Another dose of just what the rock and roll doctor ordered. Balls to the wall AC/DC with some fairly typical Angus guitar playing. The song again is nothing special but it works well enough just the same.

IF YOU WANT BLOOD YOU'VE GOT IT

Originally released as Atlantic 19212.
Released on 21st November 1978.
Produced by Harry Vanda and George Young.

With five out of eight songs from the original Let There Be Rock album this live offering could

well have been titled Let There Be Rock – Live! The album still stands out as one of the best live recordings the band has ever issued (especially as far as pure rock 'n' roll energy is concerned). There are several outstanding bootleg recordings from the Bon Scott era that are also very good. For AC/DC purists it would be a fair bet that they will always favour the Bon Scott period over Brian Johnson. This, of course, is not a slight on Brian's abilities as a singer but rather a testimony as to how irreplaceable Bon actually was.

The only down side with If You Want Blood You've Got It is that it was a single album and that the mix was not brilliant. It could easily have worked as a full blown double and it is more than likely the tapes still exist from these concerts. So how about it boys? Combine these concerts with material from the Highway To Hell tour and give us the best ever live offering from the band!

RIFF RAFF *(A Young/M Young/B Scott)*
Originally recorded for the Powerage album. One of the better tracks from the Powerage album this one became a regular show opener for AC/DC. A good start to AC/DC's first official live album and its starts in the way the album promises to continue throughout. Balls to the wall, it does not disappoint.

HELL AIN'T A BAD PLACE TO BE *(A Young/M Young/B Scott)*
Originally recorded for the Let There Be Rock album this live version really rocks. Bon's vocal is delivered in his rather raunchy vocal style and this comes across rather well live.

BAD BOY BOOGIE *(A Young/M Young/B Scott)*
Originally recorded for the Let There Be Rock album this is the second of five tracks lifted from the Let There Be Rock album. Always a popular song, live it does not disappoint especially with its extended middle section which features a guitar twiddling solo that all works very well indeed. The song then thumps back

into the coolly delivered rock piece it is. Interestingly the solo at the end is reminiscent of Ricthie Blackmore's sound during his tenure with Deep Purple in the seventies.

THE JACK *(A Young/M Young/B Scott)*
Originally recorded for the T.N.T. album and also released on the 'overseas' version of the High Voltage album this live version does not disappoint. With Bon's ability to deliver a story in a song (and this one of course is about venereal diseases). The crowd love it (the song not the diseases!) Delivered in a traditional blues fashion this song remains a favourite today.

PROBLEM CHILD *(A Young/M Young/B Scott)*
Originally recorded for the Let There Be Rock album this was a cracking track as a studio offering. As a live track it's become a classic. The crowd love it and so would almost anyone who ever heard Bon deliver this one in concert. Simple but a good one all the same.

WHOLE LOTTA ROSIE *(A Young/M Young/B Scott)*
Originally recorded for the Let There Be Rock album Whole Lotta Rosie has become one of the most enduring songs from the Bon Scott era. Still a favourite with fans today it is this (and other early) versions that really rock. Bon Scott had a very special way of delivering the goods and this track certainly shows that. It may well be the simple fact that his emotion is born from personal experience that makes his delivery so good. Angus and Malcolm absolutely rock on this one too. Classic stuff.

ROCK 'N' ROLL DAMNATION *(A Young/M Young/B Scott)*
Originally recorded for the Powerage album this was an obvious one to pick and plug on the Powerage tour. The song sounds even better in this live environment.

HIGH VOLTAGE *(A Young/M Young/B Scott)*
Originally recorded for the T.N.T. album and later released on

the 'overseas' version of the High Voltage album. For those of us who had seen the band down-under in their early years this one was always a favourite live tune. This version, although a little more polished by the years gone by doesn't fail to please. This really is classic AC/DC, simple, hard and straight to the point and the title really sums up AC/DC's music. Bon's 'talking' to the audience is a highlight for any budding rock singer.

LET THERE BE ROCK (*A Young/M Young/B Scott*)
Originally recorded as the title track for the Let There Be Rock album it is live that this track really shines. Another AC/DC classic that is as popular today as it was when Bon first wrote this clever rock and roll ditty. The song really should belong in the bible of Rock and Roll as the ultimate lesson. After all when all is said and done in music who really cares about anything else... so Let There Be Rock!

The bass playing in this version is classic AC/DC and when the guitars creep in and then rock away one is really left with little choice but to extrapolate an air guitar. Some would say it has the ending to end all endings!

ROCKER (*A Young/M Young/B Scott*)
Originally recorded for the T.N.T. album and later released on the 'overseas' version of the High Voltage album this was an early favourite with fans. Frenetic to say the least and something Chuck Berry should have been proud of!

HIGHWAY TO HELL

Originally released as Atlantic 19244.
Released on 3rd August 1979.
Produced by Robert John 'Mutt' Lange.

There is no doubting the quality of production on this album and it was that 'Americanisation' by South African producer Lange

that helped this offering crack the vital American market. And crack the American market it did in no uncertain terms. This was the last ever studio album Bon would complete with the band (although there are more than a few rumours around that he was well on the way to recording more product around the time of his death). Highway to Hell is a fitting testimony to Bon's lifestyle that is for sure but no-one can deny the rich legacy he has left in Rock and Roll.

The album shot up the US charts and in many other countries as well and it certainly cemented AC/DC as a rock and roll force to be reckoned with. Bon's untimely demise nearly put paid to that and many other bands would have cracked and folded or faded into obscurity. Not so AC/DC. Brian Johnson was recruited, Mutt Lange was retained and Back In Black was recorded. When released that too shot up the charts and the rest is history.

HIGHWAY TO HELL (*A Young/M Young/B Scott*)
Title track and a track that was destined to become an all time favourite with fans. A thudding plodder of a track it makes for a really good start to what promised to be a cracking album. Lange's use of vocal and guitar gives the track an extremely full sound. Allegedly the title refers to the band's experiences on their very first US tour and not odes to the devil as many (rather bizarre) Americans in the Bible Belt have bleated on about for years. The album deserved to sell millions alone to put the morons in place!

GIRL'S GOT RHYTHM (*A Young/M Young/B Scott*)
This is certainly one of the best tracks on the album. Bon's story is a classic set of personal anecdotes and certainly one that most of us guys can relate too. Once again Lange's use of backing vocals really sets this track apart from other fairly straight forward rockers that AC/DC were so good at delivering. Simple but one you will find yourself humming for a long long time.

WALK ALL OVER YOU *(A Young/M Young/B Scott)*
Another classic Acker-dacker classic... this one really gets up and rocks. Live this song is an absolute gem.

TOUCH TOO MUCH *(A Young/M Young/B Scott)*
Quite possibly the best track on the album Bon's vocal and the boys backing vocals give this a sound that is quite a departure from many earlier efforts. Angus's guitar is even toned down and phrased in a simple and rather commercial manner. All in all a great track.

BEATING AROUND THE BUSH *(A Young/M Young/B Scott)*
Not a bad track but by AC/DC standards this was really (very good) album filler. The riff is not unlike sounds from another rather well known band, can you work out who though?

SHOT DOWN IN FLAMES *(A Young/M Young/B Scott)*
Great riff and great chorus, if there were justice in radio play this one should have topped the charts. Simple, so simple, but a good rocker.

GET IT HOT *(A Young/M Young/B Scott)*
Another simple and rather rocky number. Became popular years later when the band resurrected it with Brian Johnson on lungs.

YOU WANT BLOOD (YOU'VE GOT IT)
(A Young/M Young/B Scott)
Title track of the previous (live) album from 1978. The track however was not included on the live offering! Simple but effective it is certainly more than your average album filler. It may well have been penned to celebrate the success of the live album or it may have been a song that was work in progress when the Powerage tour was underway. Bon's vocals however are cooler than cooler.

LOVE HUNGRY MAN *(A Young/M Young/B Scott)*
This was as near as AC/DC got to delivering a ballad on this

album. Not that it's a ballad of course but the gentle (for AC/DC) start did cause some deception when it was first released. The use of backing vocals on this one really highlights where Mutt Lange's influence had crept in and it really worked. Simple but fun this one with nice guitar interplay at the end.

NIGHT PROWLER *(A Young/M Young/B Scott)*

At nearly seven minutes this was the longest track on the album. With the tortured guitar playing at the beginning one knew one was in for a treat. Bon's whiskey soaked vocals really set this song going and although it is not unlike Ride On (from Dirty Deeds Done Dirt Cheap) and The Jack (from T.N.T.) in parts the track really does have a life of its own. It's not a song that will grab you instantly but after several listens it grabs you. A highlight on the album. Bon must have been a fan of US comedy show Mork and Mindy. Just listen to the ending.

'74 JAILBREAK

Atlantic 80178.
Released 19th October 1984.
Produced by Vanda And Young.

By 1984 AC/DC were one of the biggest rock acts on the planet and the fan base was like a pack of hungry dogs after a cut cat wanting product. The band needed something to celebrate ten years in the recording business and what better product than an EP of relatively hard to get Bon Scott tracks. The release was a welcome addition to the fans as although the songs had been previously released they were only available on expensive Australian or New Zealand imports of two of the first three albums.

Interestingly there were also a bunch of other tracks including some still hard to get B-sides that could have been added to the release had the band wanted to really give the fans value for money. The mini-album in its re-mastered form is still a welcome addition and an extremely enjoyable slice of rock done aker-dacker style. A must for any fan of the band.

JAILBREAK *(A Young/M Young/B Scott)*
Originally released on the Australasian version of the Dirty Deeds Done Dirt Cheap album from 1976. Also released as a single (with a still unreleased B-side, Fling Thing) Jailbreak should have been a huge hit and although it did make it in some rather far flung territories like Brazil it did not have the impact it deserved. In the UK the single may well have not hit its intended target because of Thin Lizzy's monster album of that year called Jailbreak which in itself was a massive hit. A stage favourite with Bon Scott on vocals, it is one of the better earlier tracks sung by Brian Johnson. If one had to make a choice to take one AC/DC song to a desert island this would certainly be my choice cut.

YOU AIN'T GOT A HOLD ON ME *(A Young/M Young/B Scott)*
From the Australasian release of the band's debut album High Voltage this song was omitted from the UK and US versions of the album of the same name. The start of this song sounds almost exactly like something Free might have recorded. That is testament in itself that this was a band on their way. The guitar sound is so much like Paul Kossoff it's spooky. This mini album is worth it for this song alone! Although the song itself is not an absolute killer the sounds the band are squeezing out of the guitars are top notch.

SHOW BUSINESS *(A Young/M Young/B Scott)*
From the Australasian release of the band's debut album High Voltage this song was omitted from the UK and US versions of the album of the same name. The song delivers a similar message and is a precursor to It's A Long Way To The Top (If You Wanna Rock 'n' Roll).

SOUL STRIPPER *(A Young/M Young)*

From the Australasian release of the band's debut album High Voltage this song was omitted from the UK and US versions of the album of the same name. Why this song was left off the non Australasian album is quite baffling as the song really does have a great grove. Simple and ever so derivative but a great listen (turn that volume right up!) all the same. Simple but effective guitar solo in this one with great rhythm punching in behind. It displayed all the things AC/DC were to exude for many years hence.

BABY, PLEASE DON'T GO *(J Williams)*

From the Australasian release of the band's debut album High Voltage this song was omitted from the UK and US versions of the album of the same name. Another song that is baffling to see why it was omitted from the 'foreign' releases. A classic Big Joe Williams number this had actually been covered with great success by Welsh rockers Budgie only two years earlier. After hearing this version it is easy to hear the obvious similarities in the execution of the song. Classic song recorded by a classic band and even today both the AC/DC and Budgie versions stand out amongst the best ever (rather numerous) covers of this song. Interestingly the song was released as a single in Australia and after much radio (and TV) airplay it reached number ten in the national charts. With this in mind it is even more baffling why it was omitted from the foreign release of High Voltage!

THE COMPILATION: BONFIRE

Released 1997 – various versions.
EW62119-2 – this version contains full Let There Be Rock concert.

A CD box set (also released in long book form as well) that contains five CDs (four in some territories) containing a fantastic

(mostly live) overview of Bon Scott's period with the band. The collection has a more than adequate booklet with liner notes and pictures. One does feel this could have been far more in depth and extensive however. None the less it gives a brief overview of Bon's career with the band. Anyone who requires more information on Bon Scott's career (not just with AC/DC either) should look no further than the comprehensive biography by Clinton Walker. The book is well written and a thoroughly enjoyable read.

DISC ONE: LIVE FROM THE ATLANTIC STUDIOS

Recorded live on December 7th 1977 at Atlantic Studios in New York City. Engineered by Jimmy Douglas. This 'in the studio' live recording was laid down after the release of Let There Be Rock and the sessions for Powerage. The sound is actually very good and the album is a rocker from start to finish. The album certainly shows how good the tracks became when worked in a live environment. The album was available as a promotional vinyl item for radio and as such limited numbers were pressed. This in turn made it a prime target for pirate and bootleg versions on both vinyl and CD.

LIVE WIRE *(A Young/M Young/B Scott)*

Originally released as a studio recording on T.N.T. in 1975. With a radio announcement introduction this live version has a quant introduction from Bon as well before rocking off into the wide blue yonder. The rhythm guitar sound on this one is to die for, for any budding guitar player. Bon's vocal, although a little rough at the start, comes across really well in this one.

PROBLEM CHILD *(A Young/M Young/B Scott)*

Originally released as a studio recording on Dirty Deeds Done Dirt Cheap in 1976 and on Let There Be Rock in 1977. Simple song and simply good. The rhythm section really rocks as well although I have to say this one always sounded better in concert (you had to be there!)

HIGH VOLTAGE *(A Young/M Young/B Scott)*
Originally released as a studio recording on T.N.T. in 1975. Running in at nearly six minutes this one really displays the band's Chuck Berry influences! Bon is in fine form and even though there is only a token 'live in the studio' audience he works his magic ever so well.

HELL AIN'T A BAD PLACE TO BE *(A Young/M Young/B Scott)*
Originally released as a studio recording on Let There Be Rock in 1977. Introducing this song Bon makes a reference that New York might just be the place this song is about. Not a bad version.

DOG EAT DOG *(A Young/M Young/B Scott)*
Originally released as a studio recording on Let There Be Rock in 1977. And again a reference to New York – it's a shame that whoever edited this for radio play left out much of Bon's chatter. Simple but fantastic guitar playing from the Youngs.

THE JACK *(A Young/M Young/B Scott)*
Originally released as a studio recording on T.N.T. in 1975. This version is extremely raw and stripped down but it works well. Bon and his audience participation are fun as well. The simple blues guitar playing on this makes it sound like you are in the room with them (as long as you play it loud!)

WHOLE LOTTA ROSIE *(A Young/M Young/B Scott)*
Originally released as a studio recording on Let There Be Rock in 1977. As Bon says, this one is about a woman who weighed three hundred and five pounds. Enough said! It rocks as it is supposed to. Always a crowd pleaser and still very popular today this version certainly shows the rawness the band had in those early years.

ROCKER *(A Young/M Young/B Scott)*

Originally released as a studio recording on T.N.T. in 1975. The radio album closer this really works well as the band hold nothing back rocking this one away. Good classic AC/DC at full throttle. The album all in all is a very good example of AC/DC with Bon in the middle of that part of their career.

DISC TWO: LET THERE BE ROCK – THE MOVIE – LIVE IN PARIS

There are two versions of this concert on CD and available in two different versions of Bonfire. One covers a complete disk (with several tracks missing) and the other is spread over a double set. Obviously the better one to have is the double set version. When this (film) soundtrack was first heard it caused a minor sensation in rock circles. Classic AC/DC tracks delivered with vibrancy only they can do. To now have the soundtrack on (re-mastered) CD is an essential addition to any fan. The live album If You Want Blood You Got it recorded during the Powerage tour was a good one. This one although not quite as good a recording really does deliver the goods. Recorded during the Highway To Hell tour it really does show AC/DC with Bon Scott at the helm as a tour de force.

Let There Be Rock – The Movie however has not yet made its debut on DVD and the only way to see this gem is on the original video release or on bootleg sources. It is of course a classic AC/DC performance and the sooner this sees the light of day on DVD the better!

PART ONE:

LIVE WIRE *(A Young/M Young/B Scott)*

Originally released as a studio recording on T.N.T. in 1975. With nearly two minutes of guitar waggling by Angus the track then starts with that ever so simple one note bass intro. Interesting eight minute live version and it is executed coolly as a show opener even if the sound quality is not brilliant.

SHOT DOWN IN FLAMES *(A Young/M Young/B Scott)*
Originally released as a studio recording on Highway To Hell in 1979. Popular live number that does work very well. Bon's vocal is a little rough on this one however.

HELL AIN'T A BAD PLACE TO BE *(A Young/M Young/B Scott)*
Originally released as a studio recording on Let There Be Rock in 1977. This number really does work well in this live version.

SIN CITY *(A Young/M Young/B Scott)*
Originally released as a studio recording on Powerage in 1978. With Sin City (dedicated to Paris) the album starts to pick up pace properly. Sin City was certainly a number that displayed (although we didn't know it at the time) the direction AC/DC would progress with on Back In Black.

WALK ALL OVER YOU *(A Young/M Young/B Scott)*
Originally released as a studio recording on Highway To Hell in 1979. Another track that with Mutt Lange's production on the studio version would show the slightly modified direction that would blast this band into orbit. Live this number worked well.

BAD BOY BOOGIE *(A Young/M Young/B Scott)*
Originally released as a studio recording on Let There Be Rock in 1977. This live version runs in at over ten minutes of blinding boogie rock. The 'crowd control' section in the middle is of course much better when you can hear this with pictures!

PART TWO:
THE JACK *(A Young/M Young/B Scott)*
Originally released as a studio recording on T.N.T. in 1975. Always a popular live number this version is certainly no exception to the rule.

HIGHWAY TO HELL *(A Young/M Young/B Scott)*
Originally released as a studio recording on Highway To Hell in 1979 the title of the aforementioned album actually sounded

even more commercial when played live. The sound quality on this part of the live recording is not brilliant however.

GIRLS GOT RHYTHM *(A Young/M Young/B Scott)*
Originally released as a studio recording on Highway To Hell in 1979. Interestingly the live tracks from Highway To Hell really did sound far more commercial than many of the earlier efforts. This track is no exception.

HIGH VOLTAGE *(A Young/M Young/B Scott)*
Originally released as a studio recording on T.N.T. in 1975. Although Bon says this track was from the first album 'they ever had' it was actually originally released on the band's second studio effort T.N.T. Live this ever so simple rocker works very well. Good one to sing along to after a few (too many) beers.

WHOLE LOTTA ROSIE *(A Young/M Young/B Scott)*
Originally released as a studio recording on Let There Be Rock in 1977. Classic AC/DC and an extremely popular number, this live version is no exception and the audience clearly love it!

ROCKER *(A Young/M Young/B Scott)*
Originally released as a studio recording on T.N.T. in 1975. A two minute forty five second song that has been extended to over three times that! This track really is boogie heaven and one can certainly see from this why the band were a true challenge to Status Quo in their rather dull late seventies period. Quo really seemed to forget who their fans really were. AC/DC on the other hand really stuck to what they knew best. This is a perfect example of just that! Get your air-guitar out. Now! Then just when you thought it had all come to an end...

T.N.T. *(A Young/M Young/B Scott)*
Originally released as a studio recording on T.N.T. in 1975. Not a bad studio track, live it usually stood out. This version is no exception. After another Angus guitar intro Bon gets the song going. Classic AC/DC.

LET THERE BE ROCK *(A Young/M Young/B Scott)*

Originally released as a studio recording on Let There Be Rock in 1977. To top it all off Bon and the boys enter the rock and roll church with Let There Be Rock. When this track was first heard it was certainly likened to the ten commandments of rock and roll and Bon and Angus really set the stage alight with this live rendition. Overall the performances are top notch however the recorded sound does let this one down a little.

DISC THREE: VOLTS

Various rarities from the Bon Scott period. In some ways it's a collection of oddities as well. There must be several albums worth of out-takes and no doubt countless live offerings collecting dust in the vaults (volts!) and hopefully these will see the light of day in a nice cohesive set of releases. In the meantime this CD is certainly better than nothing.

DIRTY EYES *(A Young/M Young/B Scott)*

Original working title of a song that eventually became Whole Lotta Rosie. The lyrics used in this early version were quite different effectively making this a different song altogether.

TOUCH TOO MUCH *(A Young/M Young/B Scott)*

Although this track has the same working title as one that appeared on Highway To Hell this is in fact a different song altogether. The track was not bad but it would have required a lot of polishing to ensure its inclusion on an album.

IF YOU WANT BLOOD YOU GOT IT

(A Young/M Young/B Scott)

The very first recording of the track that titled a live album and then appeared on Bon's last album with the band.

BACK SEAT CONFIDENTIAL *(A Young/M Young/B Scott)*

The band's first attempt at the song that would eventually become Beatin' Around The Bush which ended up on Highway To Hell.

GET IT HOT *(A Young/M Young/B Scott)*
A completely reworked version of this track eventually ended up on the Highway To Hell album. This early attempt features lyrics and music that are quite different.

SIN CITY *(A Young/M Young/B Scott)*
Live version from the 'Midnight Special'. The original studio track was included on Powerage. Although the sonic condition is not brilliant the performance is.

SHE'S GOT BALLS *(A Young/M Young/B Scott)*
A nearly eight minute live version of She's Got Balls from the Bondi Lifesaver. The original studio version was included on the debut release in Australasia entitled High Voltage recorded in 1974.

SCHOOL DAYS *(C Berry)*
A studio recording from AC/DC's second album T.N.T. which was an Australasian release only. One of the few tracks not penned by members of AC/DC this Chuck Berry classic certainly displayed the roots of AC/DC in no uncertain terms.

IT'S A LONG WAY TO THE TOP
(IF YOU WANNA ROCK 'N' ROLL) *(A Young/M Young/B Scott)*
Opening track from AC/DC's second album T.N.T. released in 1975. This track was also included on the 'overseas' version of High Voltage in 1976.

RIDE ON *(A Young/M Young/B Scott)*
Studio track lifted from the Dirty Deeds Done Dirt Cheap album released in 1976.

INTERVIEW SEGMENTS
Five minutes of anecdotes from various interviews. Interesting, if a little rough.

DISC FOUR: BACK IN BLACK
With sales of nearly forty million and counting no-one can

doubt this as a rock classic. With the other concerts and rarities on the box set this gives an immediate comparison of AC/DC of old and the new (and highly successful) Brian Johnson years. A welcome addition to the box set.

BACK IN BLACK

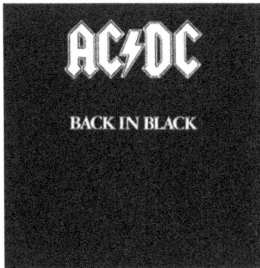

Atlantic 16018.
Released 25th July 1980.
Produced by Robert John 'Mutt' Lange.

Released on so many different versions of CD it's almost impossible to list. The latest (and greatest) version is the 2-sided dual disc version complete with thirty minutes of DVD including 'The Story Of Back In Black' which includes live and studio performances of many songs from the album along with an informative booklet.

After the untimely demise of the highly charismatic and (for AC/DC fans) iconic lead singer Bon Scott the band were thrown into a state of shock to say the least. Bon had been instrumental in their success of that there was no doubt. For most other bands it could easily have spelt the end of the road. Not so with the mighty Acker-Dacker!

Highway To Hell had proven a hit in the US and was obviously a watershed for the band and Bon and the crew had been busily rehearsing for the essential follow up album.

With Bon Scott's death the band returned to Australia for his funeral and really had no idea what they were going to do. No one to mope around Malcolm Young called his brother up and organised some rehearsals and jamming in the studio. They quickly decided to regroup and find a new lead singer. Many were tried and it was actually at Mutt Lange's suggestion that one Brian Johnson formerly of English band Geordie, and much admired by Bon himself, might fit the bill. Johnson was duly located (at the time he was working a factory line in Newcastle) and asked to audition.

No one could replace Bon Scott, that was clear to anyone who had seen him perform live but Johnson proved within a very short space of time that he was not going to attempt to replace those mighty shoes but rather try and carry on the legacy. This he seems to have done with respect and class that maybe only a Geordie can.

Most ardent fans of AC/DC split the career into two distinct periods defined by the two lead singers and because of this and Johnson's diplomatic way of dealing with this the band remains as popular as ever today.

Rehearsals progressed rapidly and the album was recorded shortly afterwards with production guru Lange in the hot seat. Lange is unusual in this role as he really does know what he's doing and there is no doubt that the success of Back In Black had as much to do with him as the band itself. No-one however could have imagined how big this album was actually going to be. To date, in the US alone it has sold close on twenty million copies and had a world-wide total of approximately forty million. Twenty five years after its release it still sells by the truckload.

As an interesting after-note it's important to point out that AC/DC were rehearsing a new album at the time of Bon Scott's death. Whether songs or parts of songs from these sessions were ever included on Back In Black is anyone's guess. Friends close to Bon say there are (although he has never been credited for any). The Young's imply not and have even released most of what they say was work in progress on the 'Volts' CD in the four CD Bonfire set (sometimes five depending on which version you have!)

Regardless of what is actually true there is no doubt that his perpetual and charismatic influence was carried over to this album in no uncertain terms, after all without him none of this would have happened.

Back In Black remains one of the classic hard rock albums of all time.

HELLS BELLS *(A Young/M Young/B Johnson)*

What a start to what was going to be a cracking album, Hells Bells said it all with its rousing entrance. This was hard edged rock and roll right from the start and the track has remained a favourite with fans ever since. Hells Bells has become (one of many from this album in fact) an anthem in no uncertain terms. The track quickly became a live favourite and was the second song from the album chosen to be included in the Stephen King horror flick Maximum Overdrive released in the mid eighties.

SHOOT TO THRILL *(A Young/M Young/B Johnson)*

With Back In Black effectively being a debut album for the new-born AC/DC they pulled out all the stops. Shoot To Thrill really rocks! Brian Johnson's hard hitting and almost (at this early stage) Zeppelinesque vocal piercing the ears and sounding similar to many of his rockier numbers with former band Geordie. Everything in this song is simple and with the volume knob cranked up to eleven no-one could fail to be impressed with its power. Classic AC/DC through and through.

WHAT DO YOU DO FOR MONEY HONEY
(A Young/M Young/B Johnson)

This is what AC/DC were masters at, heavy blues complemented by (in this case) Johnson's searing vocal. Highly repetitive this is a song you will end up humming for ages. There is nothing particularly original about anything in the track but it works regardless.

GIVIN THE DOG A BONE *(A Young/M Young/B Johnson)*

Slow driving rock this one is and an indication of the music that was to become classic AC/DC for the eighties. Great guitar in this one, and rip-roaring vocals topped off with that ever so clever Mutt Lange touch. Another track that segues immediately into the next. This simple studio trick was nothing short of genius by Lange to keep this hard rocking album flowing.

LET ME PUT MY LOVE INTO YOU

(A Young/M Young/B Johnson)

Another number where Brian Johnson's vocal past displays itself. Interestingly for AC/DC the guitar sequences even sound a little like something Geordie attempted on their 1974 release Don't Be Fooled By The Name, an album that should grace any serious 1970s rockers record collection.

The track also has a nice blues flavour and once again displays the roots of this ever so cleverly simple rock and roll band.

BACK IN BLACK *(A Young/M Young/B Johnson)*

The Young brothers openly dedicated this one to their friend and former colleague Bon Scott. With Johnson's lyrics it is not unlike something Bon Scott would have been happy delivering. Nice guitar solo in the middle section before the song thumps back into line for the chorus. This is still a favourite in the live shows today.

YOU SHOOK ME ALL NIGHT LONG

(A Young/M Young/B Johnson)

Second song on side two of the original vinyl the song was also included in the Stephen King horror epic Maximum Overdrive (this was King's first attempt at direction of one of his own films – interesting is the best way to describe this one!) The soundtrack which AC/DC supplied (and released as Who Made Who in 1986) is certainly the highlight of the movie. King has written and (had) filmed far better efforts than Maximum Overdrive that's for sure. It was cool however that he chose AC/DC, a band he seems to admire to supply the entire soundtrack.

You Shook Me All Night Long was catapulted up the charts early on in the life of Back In Black and at number thirty five on the Billboard Hot 100 chart in the US became the band's first US top forty hit.

HAVE A DRINK ON ME *(A Young/M Young/B Johnson)*
Classic rocker from the band. Definitely a song that one can stand on the bar and sing aloud after a promotion. Believe me I have seen this one in action in the city of London, although if memory serves me correctly it was after a lower manager had got his boss sacked in a financial institution. Fitting stuff. Ironically it is just this sort of simplicity that has helped make AC/DC so popular.

SHAKE A LEG *(A Young/M Young/B Johnson)*
For most bands this could be as good as it got. On an album stacked full of bone crunching numbers as Back In Black is this is as near as filler as anything was ever going to get on this release. The end section is slightly reminiscent of Let There Be Rock in parts and this would be a perfect song to have extended somewhat live. Interestingly the song also displays one of the first indications of Brian Johnson's sometimes (over) strained vocal something that has quite obviously plagued him during several live performances in recent years.

ROCK AND ROLL AIN'T NOISE POLLUTION
(A Young/M Young/B Johnson)
Nearing completion with the album Mutt Lange informed the band they needed an extra track and this was the result. The lyrics were actually ad-libbed by Brian Johnson and before many (if any) changes were done the song was recorded. It has become favourite with fans. A simple heavy number that in many ways sums up AC/DC. Great end to what has become a classic album in the rock world.

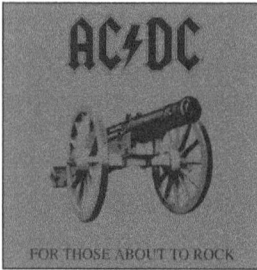

FOR THOSE ABOUT TO ROCK

Atlantic 11111.
Released 20th November 1981.
Produced by Robert John 'Mutt' Lange.

After the immense and rapid success of Back In Black it was obvious that the fans and record companies would be demanding more product... and how, quite frankly, were the band ever going to top the last album?... With For Those About To Rock of course! Although the album did not eventually sell in the same numbers the band actually sound far more cohesive and the track mix works extremely well. Quite possibly better than its predecessor even if it has never achieved the commercial success of Back In Black (very few albums ever have or ever will!) Back In Black will always overshadow this album but for true hard rockers For Those About To Rock will always remain a favourite. With Mutt Lange in the production hot chair for the third time (Highway To Hell with Bon Scott preceded Back In Black) the band certainly sounded like they felt at ease with this master of production.

Interestingly the band were scheduled into a top Paris recording studio and when they entered it and attempted to rehearse and record for the Back In Black follow up they found they just could not capture the magic. Abandoning the studio they raced off to perform for the Monsters Of Rock festival at Castle Donington in England. Playing their hearts out to a crowd of over 65,000 hard rock fans the band went down a storm. Confirming them as hard rock heroes in England right there and then.

Obviously blowing the blues away with the big gig they returned to Paris. Lange has solved the problem for recording as well by moving them to the outskirts of the French capital and hiring the Mobile One Studio from London to work in rehearsal space. This seemed to work and the band started work in earnest.

The final product was released late in 1981 and the album quickly shot up the charts and soon took the number one spot in the US charts. This was a first for AC/DC.

The band then embarked on a winter arena tour of the US and this was in fact their first full arena tour. The touring and immense success of Back In Black ensured a good response and the fans proved this by attending concerts in record numbers and buying up truckloads of the lavishly gold embossed gatefold covered For Those About To Rock. This is quite possibly one of the loudest albums you could ever listen to!

FOR THOSE ABOUT TO ROCK (WE SALUTE YOU)

(A Young/M Young/B Johnson)

Quite possibly one of the best tracks AC/DC have ever recorded and certainly the best from the Brian Johnson years to date. This is absolute classic AC/DC rocking at full throttle. This track is probably as close as you are ever going to hear Brian Johnson's vocals sounding like a tortured Robert Plant since Johnson's days with Geordie. The song should be issued with a health warning – as at full volume this one could easily bust an ear drum. Wonderful stuff! And the cannons at the end are nothing short of a masterstroke.

I PUT THE FINGER ON YOU *(A Young/M Young/B Johnson)*

A classic AC/DC rocker that Bon would have been proud of. Mutt Lange had really managed to get a melodic but rather heavy sound from the rockers and it worked ever so well. Quite possibly one of the most commercial tracks ever recorded by AC/DC. Simple but good solos, this track works very well.

LET'S GET IT UP *(A Young/M Young/B Johnson)*

A good old AC/DC chant in no uncertain terms. The playing on this is superb and Mutt Lange's influence is quite obvious. This was as near to album filler that AC/DC got to on this album. Still a good track nonetheless.

INJECT THE VENOM *(A Young/M Young/B Johnson)*
Reverting to the strong raspy vocal sound from his days in Geordie (where he often sounded like Led Zeppelin's Robert Plant) Brian Johnson really lets fly with this slow but solid rocker. The drums in this track are superb as is the barrage of guitars and bass. There is not a bad note in this song and without a shadow of a doubt you will be deafened if you listen to this one at full volume.

SNOWBALLED *(A Young/M Young/B Johnson)*
After the slow rocking of Inject The Venom the band rock it up somewhat for this one. Snowballed gives a whole new meaning to hard rock! It's simple down to earth rock and roll with a heavy metal riff and played with the apparent ease that only AC/DC can do. The guitar solos are superb in this one too.

EVIL WALKS *(A Young/M Young/B Johnson)*
Another track that could almost past for a metal anthem Evil Walks is a more than adequate album track and the guitar solo intermingled with the rumbling bass and drums in the centre section is perfect for live extension.

C.O.D. *(A Young/M Young/B Johnson)*
That ever so simple Angus start and Brian Johnson's raspy vocals really get this one going. The drums and bass are a near perfect sound. Angus and Malcolm's guitar interplay is as usual very cool.

BREAKING THE RULES *(A Young/M Young/B Johnson)*
Another slow rocker that really shows off the classiness of simple guitar playing. Angus and Malcolm Young's guitar parts are perfect. Drums and bass playing are also spot on and with Brian Johnson's Zeppelinesque sound this is a joy to listen to. Loud.

NIGHT OF THE LONG KNIVES *(A Young/M Young/B Johnson)*
This is certainly the most commercial track on the album and was in fact ahead of it time. Within months many of the early eighties metal bands had picked up on the sound and flow of tracks like this one. Still a good track to play for your neighbours.

SPELLBOUND *(A Young/M Young/B Johnson)*
Another slow heavy grinder of a track. Although AC/DC were officially a hard rock band one could question whether they had joined the heavy metal brigade with tracks like this one.

FLICK OF THE SWITCH

Atlantic 80100.
Released on August 19th 1983.
Produced by AC/DC.

This was the back to basics album for AC/DC. After the immense success of three hit albums Highway To Hell, Back In Black and For Those About To Rock We Salute You, tours of mega proportions and working with a world class producer the band wanted to try a little thing of their own. They decamped to Compass Point Studios in the Bahamas and enlisted the help of Tony Platt (who had helped Mutt Lange and the band during the recording sessions for Back In Black). Platt engineered and mixed the album. Interestingly Platt produced and engineered Uriah Heep's album with Pete Goalby less than two years later. The band were determined to record in a simple environment after the grand excesses of the immense success of the last few years. They also wanted to capture a 'live' sound which with this album they actually managed to capture near perfectly. The album does not have as full-on a production as Back In Black of For Those About To Rock and it does not have the mind-

blowing heaviness of the last two albums either. But it does have a great sound nonetheless.

This was the last album drummer Phil Rudd would record on until 1995's Ballbreaker. Flick Of The Switch is certainly the lost gem of the Brian Johnson years with AC/DC and it is a highly listenable album.

RISING POWER *(A Young/M Young/B Johnson)*
After learning the art of stacked vocals from Mutt Lange during the past two album sessions the band use the effect with gusto on this the opening track. Cool riff and some nice simple solo playing and the track really does have a 'live' sound to it.

THIS HOUSE IS ON FIRE *(A Young/M Young/B Johnson)*
A nice romper is this one! Brian Johnson certainly uses the song as a good excuse to air his lungs. Everything is simple in this track and it all works perfectly and effortlessly. This would have been perfect to use in a film soundtrack somewhere.

FLICK OF THE SWITCH *(A Young/M Young/B Johnson)*
Quite possibly the simplest riff the Young brothers have ever put together, and it works a treat. The band hadn't lost a thing producing themselves when you listen to this one. Classic AC/DC at their best. This is a fine track indeed and it really should have been the album opener.

NERVOUS SHAKEDOWN *(A Young/M Young/B Johnson)*
Could easily have resided on For Those About To Rock. Mutt Lange was a fine producer but it is obvious the band especially Angus and Malcolm had learnt a trick or two from him.

LANDSLIDE *(A Young/M Young/B Johnson)*
One of the simplest (and best) tracks on the album. If this one doesn't get you boogieing away then nothing will! This is a track I guarantee you will want to play over and over again. The guitar solos are superb. A classic example of how good AC/DC can be when in boogie mode.

GUNS FOR HIRE *(A Young/M Young/B Johnson)*

With a riff that actually sounds more Deep Purple than AC/DC this medium paced rocker works well. Brain Johnson's singing actually sounds like singing in this one in parts. This is also another good one to pull the air guitar out to.

DEEP IN THE HOLE *(A Young/M Young/B Johnson)*

With a slow almost funky (for AC/DC) start this track actually promises more than it delivers. Not that there is anything bad about it; the guitars sound great, rhythm section delivers the goods and Brian Johnson sings his heart out, it's just that the start always seems to promise more every time this track is played. Bit of an album filler.

BEDLAM IN BELGIUM *(A Young/M Young/B Johnson)*

Standard plodding rocker that actually works reasonably well while Brian Johnson yells out his story of adventures in Europe.

BADLANDS *(A Young/M Young/B Johnson)*

Someone must have been listening to Jimmy Page on Physical Graffiti just before this one was written, at least as far as the guitar playing is concerned! Quite a good track but one feels it could have had so much more done to it. This might have been more interesting with Mutt Lange's influence.

BRAIN SHAKE *(A Young/M Young/B Johnson)*

Brain shake just about says it all with this one. A nice frenetic rocker this would be a nice one to see the band resurrect for a live airing, giving it the extension treatment of course.

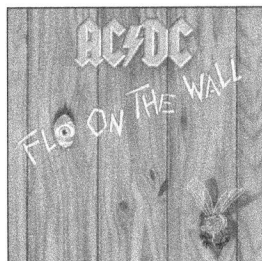

FLY ON THE WALL

Atlantic 81263.
Released 28th June 1985.
Produced by Angus Young and Malcolm Young.

After a nearly two year recording hiatus the band released Fly On The

Wall. Phil Rudd had departed to be replaced by Simon Wright. His drumming style and sound certainly changed the sound of the band a little. I'm not convinced for the better either. That is not to say he was not suited to the band but Rudd's sound and style just seemed to work better.

This time the band left the warmth of the Bahamas to record in Montreaux, Switzerland. Produced by the Young brothers it comes across as a slightly heavier album than the last offering Flick Of The Switch. The album did however seem to date and fade from peoples memories as anything special quite quickly (as did Flick Of The Switch). Both albums today however make for quite pleasant listening in parts. They actually haven't dated much at all. Not the best album by any stretch (and not as good as Flick Of The Switch) but it's not a bad one either.

FLY ON THE WALL *(A Young/M Young/B Johnson)*
The band had wanted a bigger sound after the rather flat sales of Flick Of The Switch and this song certainly shows that they achieved that. A fairly typical number for the never in fashion AC/DC. But who cared about fashion as far as this band were concerned?, They just rocked.

SHAKE YOUR FOUNDATIONS *(A Young/M Young/B Johnson)*
One of two tracks to be included in Stephen King's Maximum Overdrive this one is another typical rocker with a killer riff and raucous vocals from Brian Johnson.

FIRST BLOOD *(A Young/M Young/B Johnson)*
Another good solid rocker which has a solid bass line. The track isn't really anything special however. It's also nothing to be ashamed off either.

DANGER *(A Young/M Young/B Johnson)*
One of the best slow rock bump and grinds from AC/DC this one does highlight Brian Johnson's raucous and highly identifiable vocal sound.

SINK THE PINK *(A Young/M Young/B Johnson)*
This Fly On The Wall track was a masterpiece in group chanting in the choruses. Simple but cool guitar the track is still a good one to play.

PLAYING WITH GIRLS *(A Young/M Young/B Johnson)*
With Brian Johnson screeching in a noisy start and wonderfully choreographed rhythm guitars this one will no doubt please. What he's singing about is anyone's guess as the vocals of course are almost unintelligible (mind you that might just be the Geordie accent again!) Interesting really as at one time record company execs had wanted to replace Bon Scott in years gone by for 'not being able to decipher his singing'. The band went on of course to replace him with someone who was even harder to understand!

STAND UP *(A Young/M Young/B Johnson)*
Every album from Back In Black onwards had a 'chanting' track as inspired by Mutt Lange. This one is no exception. The track is a rather boring one all in all however. Nice couple of riffs in there though.

HELL OR HIGH WATER *(A Young/M Young/B Johnson)*
With a drum sound not unlike that of Cozy Powell at times Simon Wright struts his stuff with this one. Good riffing from the Young brothers.

BACK IN BUSINESS *(A Young/M Young/B Johnson)*
Another typical chanting rocker from the riff-meisters. A good album track where once again Brian Johnson does not sound dissimilar to Nazareth's Dan McCafferty. Nice guitar solos in this number too.

SEND FOR THE MAN *(A Young/M Young/B Johnson)*
AC/DC always liked to go out on a heavier note than most other bands and this number is no exception. Again one could be forgiven this track was not Nazareth from their Mean City

period five years earlier. Some would say this tune is classic metal. Ends on a nice long fade.

WHO MADE WHO

Atlantic 81650.
Released May 20th 1986.
Produced by Harry Vanda and George Young
*except Robert John 'Mutt' Lange * and Angus*
*Young and Malcolm Young ***

Stephen King, the master writer of the horror genre, was in 1985 a huge fan of AC/DC (which gives a completely new spin on Rocky Horror!) For one of his writing efforts entitled Maximum Overdrive King decided to take the director's chair for the movie. Some would say with mixed results (he hasn't directed a movie since – so read between the lines). Whatever, he obviously had fun and he asked AC/DC to provide the soundtrack. That they did and it is this album that was the result including the most listenable tracks from that cinematic effort. Interestingly the film does have a lot of other incidental bits from the band but these have never seen the light of day outside the actual film release on DVD.

With the movie proving a commercial flop the band were still able to capitalise on the inclusion of their music by issuing some specially made video clips (not really using pieces from the movie itself). These got a lot of MTV play and the resulting album Who Made Who shot up the charts and the band had immense success with it. Today it remains the fourth best selling AC/DC album in North America. The movie was a good old gory trip from the master of the macabre all the same which in itself gave a completely new meaning to If You Want Blood – You Got It – plenty of it in this movie! Still, it is one of those movies that once you start watching it you have to finish it just to see what happens. Even if it is crap! Stephen King has certainly written stories which have made far better films. The album today remains one of the most listenable AC/DC efforts ever, probably because of its clever mix of tracks. Cool stuff for the car stereo!

WHO MADE WHO *(A Young/M Young/B Johnson)*
The first of three (full) tracks that were written for the film it is certainly the best of the three and in fact is the most listenable track on the whole album. The track was a huge success as a single (which in turn catapulted the album up the charts) and the video was equally successful as an MTV highlight. The song since its release has remained an all time favourite with fans.

YOU SHOOK ME ALL NIGHT LONG *
(A Young/M Young/B Johnson)
The first of two tracks lifted from the multi million seller Back In Black. With Stephen King deciding to produce his first movie (with extremely mixed results) It was cool however that he chose AC/DC, a band he seems to admire to supply the entire soundtrack. This was (apparently) a favourite of his. You Shook Me All Night Long was catapulted up the charts early on in the life of Back In Black and at number thirty five on the Billboard Hot 100 chart in the US became the band's first US top forty hit.

D.T. *(A Young/M Young)*
Written especially for the Maximum Overdrive soundtrack this is actually one of the best pieces of music in the film. The drum sound is very much like something John Bonham would have thumped out and one wonders whether anyone resorted to sampling. If they didn't then this is a damn good copy of his sound. Only recorded as an instrumental this worked extremely well and it is on this album only that you will find it.

SINK THE PINK ** *(A Young/M Young/B Johnson)*
Lifted from the latest (at the time) Fly On The Wall album the track was a masterpiece in group chanting in the choruses.

Simple but cool guitar the track was a welcome inclusion in the film.

RIDE ON *(A Young/M Young/B Scott)*

Almost as good as AC/DC ever got with true blues. Lifted from the original Dirty Deeds release from 1976 with Bon Scott on vocals. The song was a good choice for the movie, even if in the film it didn't exactly play for long! (Go on go get that DVD out.)

HELLS BELLS * *(A Young/M Young/B Johnson)*

Hells Bells said it all with its rousing entrance on the Back In Black album where this track was lifted from. This was hard edged rock and roll right from the start and the track has remained a favourite with fans ever since. Hells Bells has become (one of many from this album in fact) an anthem under no uncertain terms. The track quickly became a live favourite and was the second song from Back In Black to be included in the Stephen King horror flick Maximum Overdrive released in the mid eighties.

SHAKE YOUR FOUNDATIONS **
(A Young/M Young/B Johnson)

The second of two songs from Fly On The Wall this one is another classic hard rocking rebel yell from the band. The track was one of the better numbers from the Fly On The Wall album.

CHASE THE ACE *(M Young/A Young)*

What a classic piece of rock music to drive too... very fast! The third (full) tune to be penned for the Maximum Overdrive soundtrack the track is simple to say the least. But then that's often what AC/DC is all about.. and it rocks! Wonderful guitar solo too.

FOR THOSE ABOUT TO ROCK (WE SALUTE YOU)*
(M Young/A Young/B Johnson)

Quite possibly one of the best tracks AC/DC have ever recorded and certainly the best from the Brian Johnson years so far this is absolute classic AC/DC. Needless to say it was an appropriate piece to include on the soundtrack. This track is probably as close as you are ever going to hear Brian Johnson's vocals sounding like a tortured Robert Plant since Johnson's days with Geordie. The song should be issued with a health warning – as at full volume this one could easily bust an ear drum.

BLOW UP YOUR VIDEO

Atlantic 81828.
Released 1st February 1988.
Produced by Harry Vanda and George Young.

It appeared in the early part of the eighties that AC/DC could do no wrong as far as the record companies were concerned. By the mid nineties many involved had started to change their tune. AC/DC in a word (well an album actually) wiped out the idea that they were a declining force with the release of Who Made Who. Simon Wright was in the drum seat for his second outing for the three tracks they recorded for the aforementioned project and he was also present for the Blow Up Your Video recording sessions over two years later. The band were on a revival wave but there were clearly things amiss. Malcolm Young was fighting alcohol addiction and the band had to deal with this sometimes with him around, sometimes not.

The album was also the first full album since the seventies for which George Young and Harry Vanda sat in the producer's chair. They had however produced the three new tracks for the Who Made Who release in 1985. This made Blow Up Your Video the first full blown project that they produced with Brian Johnson on vocals. All in all it works very well. The album is a simple hard rocking no frills affair. Just what the doctor ordered for a period in the late eighties that was full of big hair bands trying to write meaningful things (yeah right!).

This was the last album to feature Simon Wright on drums. He was replaced for the next (1990) project by Chris Slade formerly of Manfred Mann's Earthband and Uriah Heep. Nineteen songs were attempted in the French studios where the album was recorded. Ten made the grade. Turn up the volume and Blow Up Your Ears. Enjoy.

HEATSEEKER *(M Young/A Young/B Johnson)*
One of the best tracks from the band in years, this one was a mixture of pure commercialism and out and out rock and roll. Built around a catchy hook it was fairly obvious this one was going to do very well. Brian Johnson's gritty vocals have rarely been better in his time with AC/DC.

THAT'S THE WAY I WANNA ROCK N ROLL
(M Young/A Young/B Johnson)
Nice riff and clever offbeat drumming start this one off very well. It turns into a good AC/DC rocker. Not the best on the album but not the worst either.

MEANSTREAK *(M Young/A Young/B Johnson)*
For AC/DC this really was quite a slinky number. It has a good groove and once again Brian Johnson's vocals really have some depth, once again it does actually sound like Nazareth's Dan MaCafferty had joined the band such was the similarity in style! Even the guitar style was not unlike something Manny Charlton (Nazareth's original guitarist) might have laid down.

GO ZONE *(M Young/A Young/B Johnson)*
Simple bass line with some clever stutter guitar overlaid with Brian Johnson's (sounds like whiskey soaked) vocal. The track doesn't actually seem to do very much but it works all the same. Clever. The lyrics however are somewhat simpler, well downright basic actually!

KISSIN' DYNAMITE *(M Young/A Young/B Johnson)*

Lyrically this album is certainly based around sex, sex and more sex. This song is no exception. Basic (in more ways than one) rock song that for AC/DC is good album filler.

NICK OF TIME *(M Young/A Young/B Johnson)*

A cool rocker that doesn't half borrow hooks from a number of other songs. Not all AC/DC either. See if you can pick which ones. A catchy number that you will find yourself playing over and over.

SOME SIN FOR NUTHIN' *(M Young/A Young/B Johnson)*

Dan sings again! Whoops I mean Brian! The vocal likeness is uncanny here. The song is a slow rocker with some simple (but nice) guitar playing.

RUFF STUFF *(M Young/A Young/B Johnson)*

Another rebel yell about sex. Same old, same old really this one. It does have a clever hook in the song however but it never seems to quite hit the mark.

TWO'S UP *(M Young/A Young/B Johnson)*

Another rude lyric from Brian Johnson, quite possibly from his experiences of a threesome. God forbid the thought for all us blokes! It's a bit of a plodder but it has a nice ending.

THIS MEANS WAR *(M Young/A Young/B Johnson)*

Typical (frenetic) AC/DC with very cool riffs and hook. Ever so simple but this is one you will end up playing a lot and it's a great way to finish what is in fact an enjoyable album. Brian Johnson's vocals on this one once again confirm his similarity in style to Nazareth's Dan McCafferty. Uncanny quite frankly. Maybe AC/DC had been playing No Mean City on the tour bus prior to recording this album!

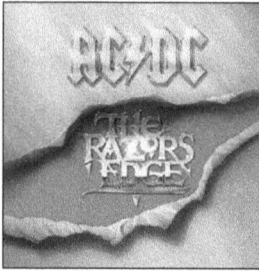

THE RAZORS EDGE

Atco 91413.
Released 21st September 1990.
Produced by Bruce Fairburn.

Interestingly The Razors Edge has some cracking rock tracks but the style of production used to record these is actually quite different from anything AC/DC had done prior to this. The guitars have a lot of finesse all of the time and the vocals are far more laid back in the mix than productions by Mutt Lange, Vanda and Young or the band themselves. Brilliant (now late) producer as Fairburn was it actually does take away a lot of the rawness that AC/DC has traditionally relied on. This album is no exception. Although it sold by the truckload quite frankly the album is missing that vital (raw) ingredient. To top that off there are several songs that are quite frankly nothing short of boring.

In 1989 the band decamped to Little Mountain Studios in Vancouver, Canada to record the album with Fairburn and by 1990 had delivered a package of very good songs. This time however there were some major changes to the scenario. Brian Johnson had not contributed to the lyrics (mainly due to a difficult divorce) and the Young brothers had attempted to carry off this task themselves. It worked and in fact although there are plenty of sex and roll numbers the album is not quite so full of it.

The other major change was the departure of Simon Wright on drums and the entrance of veteran (and highly skilled) drummer Chris Slade. Slade has previously played (extensively) with Manfred Mann's Earthband (interestingly alongside Colin Pattenden who in earlier years had been considered as a bass player for AC/DC). Slade has also recorded the rather infamous Uriah Heep album Conquest (where his drumming was once again quite exceptional – quite possibly the best thing on that album!) Slade certainly brought a different style (and consequently) a different feel to the recording.

THUNDERSTRUCK *(M Young/A Young)*
Cracking start to the album and from the first listen one knew this would become an AC/DC staple. Clever rhythm riff and the song is set alight. Simple and clever as AC/DC so often are.

FIRE YOUR GUNS *(M Young/A Young)*
Fairly typical AC/DC rocker. It's well played and as such not a bad number but then again it's not really anything special. Album filler.

MONEYTALKS *(M Young/A Young)*
Whoever thought AC/DC would write many songs as commercial as this one. It's actually a very laid back rocker from the boys and has a slight blues feel to it. Great hook and a highly recognisable song once you have heard it… er once!

THE RAZORS EDGE *(M Young/A Young)*
Quite an unusual track for the band to attempt and it works extremely well. This actually does sound like AC/DC attempting someone else's (very good) song! Chris Slade's drumming in this one is outstanding.

MISTRESS FOR CHRISTMAS *(M Young/A Young)*
Here we go.. returning to circa 1975! The track is like the AC/DC of old and it works ever so well. Interesting Christmas tidings are sung here and I'll bet you will never see it alongside Bing Crosby or Slade on a Christmas compilation!

ROCK YOUR HEART OUT *(M Young/A Young)*
Another clever (drumming) track. The use of phased stereo (remember that from the sixties!) by Fairburn actually works very well. This is a track that will grow on you a lot after a few listens and remains today as one of the more interesting tracks ever recorded by AC/DC with Brian Johnson.

ARE YOU READY *(M Young/A Young)*

Bit of (not so good) filler here. This one sounds a little too much like one of the big hair bands that had been so popular a few years earlier. Less than average filler.

GOT YOU BY THE BALLS *(M Young/A Young)*

Fairly standard filler this one is as well. Not that there is anything that is terrible about it but neither is it exactly a riveting song. If you have an ipod you can skip it!

SHOT OF LOVE *(M Young/A Young)*

Those little stereo tricks are used on this one again and that is quite possibly the best thing about the recording. Good (and typical) strong AC/DC riff but it really fails to do the things that they used to be able to pull off in the past. Filler and nothing more.

LET'S MAKE IT *(M Young/A Young)*

Let's Make It was the title. Shame the band didn't with this one. Three (relative) lemons in a row! The band were sounding tired to say the least on this one.

GOODBYE AND GOOD RIDDANCE TO BAD LUCK
(M Young/A Young)

This album really did sell by the truck load but it was quite obviously not on the back of some of the latter tracks on the album. Quite frankly this one says it all if they were to continue issuing tosh like this one. This would have to rate as one of the all time worst tracks recorded by the band. Ever.

IF YOU DARE *(M Young/A Young)*

With this they actually redeem themselves (in a fashion). Although it's not exactly typical AC/DC it's not a bad track to have on the tail end of an album. It could have been worse, they could have ended it with any one of the three previous tracks.

LIVE

Atco 92212.
Originally released on 27th October 1992.
Produced by Bruce Fairburn.

With the release of The Razors Edge the same line-up that recorded that album went out on a mammoth world tour to promote the album. The concerts for this the second official live album (excluding radio shows and box set additions) were all recorded during the series of tours promoting Razors Edge. Once again produced by Bruce Fairburn this effort really does capture the heavy and all encompassing rocky sound that AC/DC are famous for, something Fairburn didn't really manage to capture on the Razors Edge studio recordings. The sound is so good on this live recording that it seems pretty obvious that there was a fair amount of in the studio 'fixing' after the event. Not that that is wrong, after all one of the finest live albums of the seventies (Thin Lizzy's – Live and Dangerous) was unashamedly 'fixed' in that manner by producer Tony Visconti in 1978.

Two versions of the album exist. A single CD version and a double set (as featured here). Quite frankly for any lover of the band it is better to shell out the extra few bucks for the double set.

With veteran drummer Chris Slade occupying the drum stool this live chronicle really does show what he can do. In the studio he is an exceptional drummer (although The Razors Edge studio sessions don't really allow him to display his wares too much), live his performance is exemplary.

From a technical point of view there is only one major flaw on this live album and that is the failure of the songs to segue. Several times one live song fades out and another fades in. This is obviously because the recordings of several tracks are from different concerts. In saying that it is usually nicer to 'mix' these together, after all other recording work was done to the recordings in the studio after the event in all probability and this would have been a nice touch for anyone wanting to listen to the album in one sitting (mind you that task would no doubt make you deaf!)

The (double set version) of Live over all is a more than acceptable record of a classic band in action on the stage.

DISK ONE:
THUNDERSTRUCK *(A Young/M Young)*
Originally released as a studio recording on Razors Edge in 1990. A good opener and one the band were keen to use as they were touring to promote The Razors Edge album.

SHOOT TO THRILL *(A Young/M Young/B Johnson)*
Originally released as a studio recording on Back In Black in 1980. This is as good a version as you are ever likely to hear of this popular Back In Black track.

BACK IN BLACK *(A Young/M Young/B Johnson)*
Originally released as a studio recording on Back In Black in 1980. Again another good recording. Interestingly many of the tracks have been heard on the several live DVDs that have been made available and the Brian Johnson based tracks generally sound better on this release than the DVD releases. This may well have been because Bruce Fairburn and Co. 'tidied' up a few things in the studio.

SIN CITY *(A Young/M Young/B Scott)*
Originally released as a studio recording on Powerage in 1978. Originally this was sung by Bon Scott of course and this is the first of 'his' tracks to be aired on this live offering with Brian Johnson on vocals.

WHO MADE WHO *(A Young/M Young/B Johnson)*
Originally released as a studio recording on Who Made Who

in 1986 and on the Maximum Overdrive soundtrack. Cracking track and live it actually sounds even better here than on the original studio release.

HEATSEEKER *(A Young/M Young/B Johnson)*
Originally released as a studio recording on the Blow Up Your Video album from 1998. One of the best tracks from the aforementioned album this one really rocks. Live this one is always a joy to hear and this version is no exception.

FIRE YOUR GUNS *(A Young/M Young)*
Originally released as a studio recording on The Razors Edge recorded in 1990. This is the second track on this double outing from Razors Edge and live it sounds far better than on the studio release. The band let loose on this one and that was something that sometimes didn't translate with the Fairburn produced studio effort this one originated from.

JAILBREAK *(A Young/M Young/B Scott)*
Originally released as a studio recording on the original Australasian Dirty Deeds Done Dirt Cheap from 1976 (in the US it was released on the Jailbreak mini album in 1984. This version is a very good one. Not as good as Bon ever sang it, granted. But a very good effort nonetheless. The track is worth it for the guitar solos (at the beginning of the song and for an extended period within the performance. Angus and Malcolm are in top form and at nearly fifteen minutes this is an air guitarist's heaven. Chris Slade's solid drumming is stunning and it is live that he really shines.

THE JACK *(A Young/M Young/B Scott)*
Originally released as a studio recording on the Australian release T.N.T. in 1975 and on the 'overseas' release of High Voltage in 1976. This was one of Bon's signature tunes that Brian Johnson has managed to make a god job of. Modern fans (that's post 1980 by the way!) won't know any different from

live gigs but those of us that managed to see the band in the good old seventies know better! Still it is better to hear it live than not.

THE RAZORS EDGE *(A Young/M Young)*
Originally released as a studio recording on The Razors Edge in 1990. Third track from this album to be picked for the live treatment. Dan McCafferty joined AC/DC you say? Well no he didn't, but listening to this track one might wonder. Heavy and very cool live version.

DIRTY DEEDS DONE DIRT CHEAP
(A Young/M Young/B Scott)
Originally released as a studio recording on Dirty Deeds Done Dirt Cheap in 1976 (1981 in the US). Another one of Bon's that Brian Johnson has managed to translate well. The band are in fine (and very heavy) form on this one.

MONEYTALKS *(A Young/M Young)*
Originally released as a studio recording on The Razors Edge in 1990. Fourth track to be lifted from the Razors Edge sessions. The song was a hit and always went down well with fans. It is certainly one of the most commercial tracks that the band have ever recorded and it works very well live.

DISK TWO:
HELLS BELLS *(A Young/M Young/B Johnson)*
Originally released as a studio recording on Back In Black in 1980. Not a bad version of this classic number however there are certainly better versions kicking around on video. Always popular live it is very hard to beat the Mutt Lange produced studio classic.

ARE YOU READY *(A Young/M Young)*
Originally released as a studio recording on The Razors Edge in 1990. They had to push the current album didn't they? Mediocre version of a mediocre track.

THAT'S THE WAY I WANNA ROCK 'N' ROLL
(A Young/M Young/B Johnson)
Originally released as a studio recording on Blow Up Your Video in 1988. Now this one works way better live than the original studio version. Great drumming from Chris Slade.

HIGH VOLTAGE *(A Young/M Young/B Scott)*
Originally released as a studio recording on T.N.T. in 1975 and on the 'overseas' version of High Voltage in 1976. A more than proficient version. This track has always worked well with Brian Johnson at the vocal stand.

YOU SHOOK ME ALL NIGHT LONG
(A Young/M Young/B Johnson)
Originally released as a studio recording on Back In Black in 1980. Classic Brian Johnson led track. Works very well live.

WHOLE LOTTA ROSIE *(A Young/M Young/B Scott)*
Originally released as a studio recording on Let There Be Rock in 1977. This live outing is recorded much faster than the original and actually sounds more like Led Zeppelin attempting a rock and roll track than almost anything AC/DC have ever recorded before. So frenetic is this version you will even get tired listening to it!

LET THERE BE ROCK *(A Young/M Young/B Scott)*
Originally released as a studio recording on Let There Be Rock in 1977. Although this was always one of Bon's most memorable tracks Brian Johnson has managed to carry this off extremely well. This version is an epic twelve minutes plus of manic rock and roll sermon. This a track fit for any air guitarists, air bass players and air drummers! Your friends will think you are nuts but who really cares! This one will probably get even the most subdued going!

BONNY *(Traditional; arranged by A Young/M Young)*
Not previously released. A lovely little guitar piece displaying

the Young brothers' Celtic roots. Nice touch to pick one called Bonny. A cool addition to the live set.

HIGHWAY TO HELL *(A Young/M Young/B Scott)*

Originally released as a studio recording on Highway To Hell in 1979. A top notch Bon Scott penned number given the treatment by Brian Johnson. Nice to hear but not as good as the live versions that were delivered so vigorously by Bon in the past.

T.N.T. *(A Young/M Young/B Scott)*

Originally released as a studio recording on T.N.T. in 1975 and the 'overseas' version of High Voltage in 1976. Another classic number given the Johnson treatment. Again not as good as Bon ever delivered it but a great live version all the same.

FOR THOSE ABOUT TO ROCK (WE SALUTE YOU)
(A Young/M Young/B Johnson)

Originally released as a studio recording on For Those About To Rock in 1981. Now this one is a different story. Classic Johnson led AC/DC and the band at their absolute finest. This has got to be one of the best hard rock songs the band have ever delivered. Live it will make your jaw rattle!

BALLBREAKER

Epic EPC 5173842.
Released 1995.
Produced by Rick Rubin and co-produced by Mike Fraser.

In early 1993 with Phil Rudd back in the drum chair the band commenced work on a single for The Last Action Hero movie. Entitled Big Gun producer Rick Rubin was called in to perform the production duties. Released with a live version of Back In Black, Big Gun was an ok single for an ok movie. Filming

for the video commenced in May of '93 and the soundtrack was released in July of 1993.

Work commenced in early 1994 preparing a new album and recording commenced in October 1994 with Rubin being retained for production duties. These sessions never saw the light of day and the band relocated to Ocean Way Studios in LA with Mike Fraser helping Rubin out with production duties. Released in October 1995 the album reached number four in the US album charts and certified platinum.

A top producer in the field of rock and rap he may be, but Rubin does anything but deliver the goods on this offering. Quite frankly the band did a far better job producing themselves (listen to Flick Of The Switch). The album has moments that should work very well (well actually some do) but there are other parts where quite frankly it gets too fiddly and the plot seems to get lost. Many have raved about this album but quite frankly I don't get it! Not that it's terrible, far from it. In fact it is a better album than many a band would strive to produce for years and years. But for AC/DC quite frankly it is a disappointment. There are a couple of good numbers on it however. They didn't use Rick Rubin again after this one and I for one can understand why. He really didn't seem to bring anything to the party they couldn't have done themselves. Stick to Harry Vanda and / or George Young or better still they should try and see if Mutt Lange would give it another shot. Now that would be interesting.

However the album shipped by the truckload so something must have worked.

HARD AS A ROCK *(A Young/M Young)*
A typical AC/DC rocker that delivers the goods (watch out girls!) The track is a return to the real simplicity of old and the track is a fun one.

COVER YOU IN OIL *(A Young/M Young)*

Another sex laden lyric. The track works reasonably well but isn't anything special.

THE FUROR *(A Young/M Young)*

One of the better tracks on the album this has a strong rhythm to it. No doubt if one rewrote the title (just a little) it might go down well in parts of Germany. Or not.

BOOGIE MAN *(A Young/M Young)*

This no doubt will work very well in a live environment as it is a slow boogie that leaves a lot of opportunity for guitar theatrics. This studio version however is actually quite boring. Album filler.

THE HONEY ROLL *(A Young/M Young)*

Another slow rocker. Again nothing really special although there are moments of promise with the guitar in the latter parts of the song.

BURNIN' ALIVE *(A Young/M Young)*

The song starts with promise but quite frankly it is Brian Johnson's rather appalling vocal that really lets this one down. Total tosh with the exception of the odd guitar break (and those are painfully short in this one).

HAIL CAESAR *(A Young/M Young)*

Simple but clever riff starts this one. But once again it almost seems to fall apart just as it gets started. The chorus is rather cool however even if the track doesn't quite seem to get there. Interestingly this is something that, had Bon Scott been around to attempt, it may well have worked. The track is one of the better on the album however.

LOVE BOMB *(A Young/M Young)*

Another relatively weak track. It has its moments however. Like a lot of tracks on the album it really suffers from a sub-standard vocal and this is something that may well stem from 'different' production rather than the singer himself.

CAUGHT WITH YOUR PANTS DOWN *(A Young/M Young)*
A strong riff and a fairly straightforward rocker this track is one of the better tracks on the album. The guitar sound is quite interesting as well.

WHISKEY ON THE ROCKS *(A Young/M Young)*
The best thing about this number is that interesting guitar sound otherwise it is yet another rather weak number.

BALLBREAKER *(A Young/M Young)*
Well this one is a cracking track. Everything that is good about (modern) AC/DC is in this one. Nice way to end an album even if it would have made a better album opener than anything else on the disk.

STIFF UPPER LIP

Epic 5173852.
Released 2000.
Produced by George Young.

The band entered The Warehouse Studios in Vancouver (owned by Brian Adams. The studio, not Vancouver!) With George Young in the production chair the sessions see seventeen tracks recorded, twelve of which make the album.

Right from track one it is apparent that the band feel more together in the studio and George Young's production (probably more like non-interference and sensible recommendations) shines above the last effort Ballbreaker. The album like Ballbreaker does lack a little something from earlier efforts and this may be something as simple as the fact that only Angus and Malcolm Young were in on the writing, Brian Johnson once again being omitted. In fact the latter part of the album would easily rate as some of the most boring material the band have ever let escape from the studio. Not an album one will play over and over again. Not that I would write AC/DC off just yet. They still sell albums by the truckload and even if these last few albums (Ballbreaker and this one, Stiff Upper Lip) lack the spark of earlier tour de forces you can be almost certain the boys will pull the proverbial rabbit out of the hat and deliver a good old rock and roller of an album. Fingers crossed then.

STIFF UPPER LIP (A Young/M Young)

One of the best tracks to be recorded by AC/DC in many a year. Tongue in cheek (or on the upper lip!) lyrics make this one a fun track to listen to. The guitar solos are simple but effective and the track rocks along quite nicely.

MELTDOWN (A Young/M Young)

A slower romp where the track sounds like it could have come from The Flick Of The Switch sessions.

HOUSE OF JAZZ (A Young/M Young)

One of the best tracks on the album, this is a really typical AC/DC in go-slow mode. The guitar breaks are classic.

HOLD ME BACK (A Young/M Young)

Simplicity rules and this one is no exception. The track does hark back to days of old but it doesn't capture the spark that so many of those earlier tracks managed to do.

SAFE IN NEW YORK CITY (A Young/M Young)

This is more like it. The band rock on this one. Repetitive but it does work very well. It also sound likes something Nazareth might have attempted a few years earlier, most noticeable in this song is the similarity to Brian Johnson's vocal to that of Dan McCafferty of Nazareth.

CAN'T STAND STILL (A Young/M Young)

Another little rocker that harks back to days of old.

CAN'T STOP ROCK 'N' ROLL *(A Young/M Young)*

Like a number of tracks on this album the vocal sounds extremely strained. It works on a few songs but can get tiresome after a while. This is one of those rather tiresome numbers. Filler.

SATELLITE BLUES *(A Young/M Young)*

Not a bad track and one that does come across live very well.

DAMNED *(A Young/M Young)*

Album filler, what else can one say about this one?

COME AND GET IT *(A Young/M Young)*

Another slow plodder where everything from the benign 'come and get it' lyric to Brian Johnson's rather lacklustre performance leave this one more than a little cold.

ALL SCREWED UP *(A Young/M Young)*

All Screwed Up kind of sums it up for many of the later tracks on this rather average album.

GIVE IT UP *(A Young/M Young)*

At least this one rocks a little bit. Basically though many of the tracks just seem to lack ideas that give them spark.

NB: It should be noted that the information regarding releases and release dates is as accurate as possible. As complete a picture as possible has been compiled but I have no doubt there are items that may be missing. The descriptions of songs and performances are personal opinion only.

Robert M Corich, October 2005

ABOUT CODA BOOKS

Most Coda books are edited and endorsed by Emmy Award winning filmmaker and concert promoter Bob Carruthers. Over the last 20 years Bob has filmed and promoted tours, concerts and made documentaries all over Britain and Europe in venues ranging from Hammersmith Odeon to Murrayfield Stadium, with artists such as Bryan Adams, Spandau Ballet, Jethro Tull, Status Quo and Katherine Jenkins.

The 'Uncensored On the Record' series explores the careers of many of music's greatest legends, encompassing a wide range of genres including classic rock, pop, heavy metal, punk, country, classical and soul.

For more information visit **www.codabooks.com**.

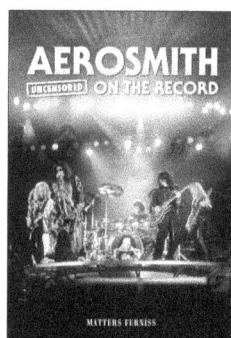

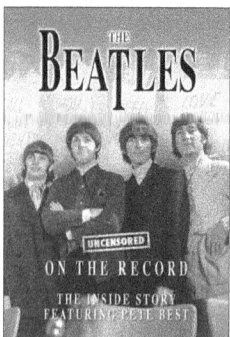

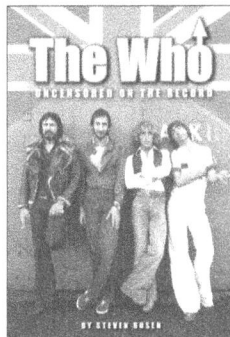